CIVIL WAR!

America Becomes One Nation

James I. Robertson, Jr.

ALFRED A. KNOPF : NEW YORK

THIS IS A BORZOI BOOK PUBLISHED BY ALFRED A. KNOPF, INC.

Text copyright © 1992 by James I. Robertson, Jr.
Maps copyright © 1992 by Jim Kemp and Anita Karl.
All rights reserved under International and Pan-American Copyright
Conventions. Published in the United States by Alfred A. Knopf,
Inc., New York, and simultaneously in Canada by Random House
of Canada Limited, Toronto. Distributed by Random House, Inc.,
New York.

Manufactured in the United States of America.
Book design by Mina Greenstein.   1   2   3   4   5   6   7   8   9   10

Library of Congress Cataloging-in-Publication Data
Civil War! : America becomes one nation / by James I. Robertson, Jr.
    p.   cm. Includes bibliographical references, glossary, chronology,
            and index.
Summary: Examines the causes, major battles, military leaders, and
            effects of the American Civil War.
1. United States—History—Civil War, 1861–1865—Juvenile liter-
    ature. [1. United States—History—Civil War, 1861–1865.]
        I. Title.   E468.R715   1992   973.7—dc20   91-19177
    ISBN 0-394-82996-4 (trade)   ISBN 0-394-92996-9 (lib. bdg.)

Photo research by the author.
Additional picture research by Carousel Research, Inc.

ADDITIONAL PHOTO CREDITS:
Front cover: Detail from *First at Vicksburg* by H. Charles McBarron, Jr.
(The Granger Collection); map of battlefield at
Dinwiddie, Virginia, March 1865 (private collection).
Back cover: Union and Confederate national, division, and
corps flags (private collection).
Page 50: Springfield rifle-musket (Smithsonian Institution).
Page 114: Confederate dead at Antietam (Library of Congress).

ACKNOWLEDGMENTS

THE J. AMBLER JOHNSTON RESEARCH FUND and a grant associated with the C. P. Miles Professorship, both at Virginia Polytechnic Institute and State University, defrayed some of the expenses incurred in producing the text and illustrations. I am deeply appreciative of such assistance.

Several schoolteacher-friends, devoted to their calling, volunteered at the outset to read the finished manuscript and to make suggestions for its improvement. Their generosity and their help were encouragements for which I shall always be grateful. My "loyal troops" in this project were Jean L. Cervone of Levittown, Pennsylvania, Monie Chase of Deerfield, Massachusetts, Ann Ferrell and Frank R. Moseley of Blacksburg, Virginia, and Phyllis Long of Lawrence, Kansas. Similar thanks go to Jennifer Evans and Cathy Vogel of the Atlanta Historical Society.

To the dozens of schoolchildren who not only read this work in manuscript form but also sent me individual letters and comments, my indebtedness is long-lasting—as evidenced by the number of their suggestions incorporated into the text.

Illustrations are very important in a work such as this. Corrine P. Hudgins of the Museum of the Confederacy, Richmond, Virginia, and George S. Hobart of the Library of Congress, Washington, D.C., were exceedingly helpful in pointing the way to many of the photographs reproduced for this book.

Regina Kahney, editorial director of nonfiction at Knopf, shared my excitement over this project from the beginning. Her editorial skills throughout made this study a far better work than it would have been.

She proved again that a good editor always makes a writer look better.

Over the years many friends asked that I undertake a basic study of the Civil War for young readers as well as for adults who wanted a simple history of the 1861–1865 conflict. My wife, Libba, was always in the front row of that group. I earnestly hope that *Civil War!* meets with their satisfaction.

JAMES I. ROBERTSON, JR.

CONTENTS

INTRODUCTION

United We Stand

"CIVIL WAR! CIVIL WAR! We're going to war!" screamed American newspapers in the spring of 1861.

Everyone seemed excited and joyful. Men rushed to join the armies: they were afraid the war might end before they could be part of it. Women tearfully watched them go. Many of them secretly wished that they too could be soldiers. "God is on our side!" Northerners and Southerners alike shouted. Each side agreed: this was going to be a short, clean, nice war—a quick contest in which there would be much chance for glory and little chance of being killed or wounded.

As a matter of fact, the Civil War became the most important event in the history of the United States. It lasted four long years. It began with old-fashioned infantry charges and cavalry attacks. It ended with massed firepower and the greatest slaughter of soldiers the world had seen up to that time. No war in world history between 1815 and 1914 was as large or as far-reaching in its results.

More than fifty major battles and 5,000 minor actions took place. The number of Americans who died in the Civil War—618,000 soldiers and perhaps as many as 100,000 civilians—is greater than the total number who died in the American Revolution, War of 1812, Mexican War, Spanish-American War, World War I, World War II, Korean War, Vietnam War, and Gulf War *combined*.

Just about every family in the nation had a father, son, brother, nephew, or cousin in the armies of North or South. One of every four of those Civil War soldiers died. More men perished from sickness and disease than were killed in action. This war was a particularly bitter, sad, and tragic conflict.

Beyond the horror and the killing, the Civil War brought an end to three heated controversies about the future of our country. First, Northern victory meant that there would be a permanent union of states. In the 1780s, our forefathers had created a nation, to be sure, but the various sections were so different and disconnected from one another that the "United States" was a name more than it was a fact.

Second, the Civil War determined that the rebuilt country would be a nation with a strong federal government (a federation) rather than a country of powerful states loosely held together by a weak federal government (a confederation).

Finally, the Civil War settled the issue of whether America was to be a land where, according to the Declaration of Independence, "all men are created equal," or whether it was to continue after 1860 as the largest slaveholding nation in the world.

The U.S. Constitution, ratified in 1788, failed to make those directions of government clear for later generations. Within seventy years after the formation of the "United States of America," the Northern dream of freedom and the Southern desire for slavery had become so strong that the two sections seemed to have little in common. By 1860, they were on a collision course. Americans could not seem to find a peaceful solution. Thus, when talking failed, shooting began.

It should not have happened that way, but it did. The Civil War will always stand as a terrible reminder of what can take place in a democracy when good people fail to sit down and calmly settle differences of opinion.

Why armed conflict between North and South took place, how the struggle was fought, and the many changes it brought about to the new nation are the subjects of this book. In brief fashion, this study seeks to explain how a young country suddenly began fighting itself. The book describes the major military campaigns as well as the political leaders and military commanders who directed the war from opposite sides. Some chapters discuss what it was like to be a Civil War soldier, how the navies performed in the struggle, the sacrifices made by women, and the amazing legacy left to America.

The Civil War touched every part of American life. It was our national revolution. From it came the strong and united nation the world knows.

CIVIL WAR!

America Becomes One Nation

1

King Cotton and His Slaves

THE GREAT DREAM that brought the first waves of settlers to our land was opportunity, not unity. Colonists by the hundreds of thousands braved the winds and waves of the Atlantic Ocean to step ashore all along our vast coast. Differing terrains and climates led people to pursue differing ways of life. No one was overly concerned that the cold and rocky area of New England became a center for town life, shipping, and commercial interests, while the warm, fertile fields of the South produced a heavily rural society. The midwestern and southwestern sections were likewise unalike in many ways. As a result, the "United States" began as a nation that was the sum of its parts rather than as a country whose people had a common outlook.

In time, the South became the section with the strongest identity. It became so by choice. While the rest of the young nation worked for improvements, progress, and the future, the Southern states looked toward tradition, stability, and the past. Agriculture was the basic way of life in the area below Maryland, cotton was the leading money crop, and slavery was the labor system on which everything rested.

In 1790, however, cotton planters were facing a crisis. Harvesting a crop meant that the cotton fibers had to be carefully removed from the sticky seeds by hand. It took one slave a whole day to collect a pound of cotton lint. Each field of cotton yielded three pickings. One picking was barely completed before new blooms appeared and the plants had to be picked again. Sometimes a third of a crop decayed before the fibers could be collected.

A Northern teacher and amateur inventor named Eli Whitney came to the South's rescue. In 1793, while he was in Georgia, Whitney built a simple device with spoked wheels that quickly separated fibers from seeds. Whitney's engine (the "cotton gin," as it became known) brought new life to cotton growing. At the same time, the development of the textile industry in both New England and England created a huge demand for cotton.

Southern planters responded by growing more and more cotton. In every ten years from 1800 to 1860, cotton production doubled. Soon the

LEFT: *It took Eli Whitney only a few weeks to perfect a cotton engine, or "cotton gin," as it came to be called. A single gin could separate the cotton fibers from the sticky seed a hundred times faster than a slave doing the task by hand. (Library of Congress)*
BELOW: *Slaves on a Beaufort, South Carolina, plantation are cleaning picked cotton before feeding it into a cotton gin. (Museum of the Confederacy)*

South was economically the most important section of the United States. Cotton accounted for two-thirds of America's revenue and reigned over the national economy. "Cotton Is King!" was more than a proud cry; it became a national fact.

With the "Cotton Kingdom" spreading across the Southern states, America became the largest slaveholding nation in the world. Growing cotton demanded many field workers. Some people began saying, "The South was built on the backs of blacks."

The Cotton Kingdom extended from South Carolina and western Tennessee to the Gulf regions of Texas. Great plantations came into being, with cotton fields spreading in every direction. Yet two weaknesses existed in the system.

First, cotton cultivation became bigger, but not better. Few new tools or equipment appeared after Whitney's invention. The Old South placed its future in hand labor and did not become part of the North's great modernizing movement known as the Industrial Revolution.

Second, great cotton fields required a huge labor force. Black slaves were that labor supply. It was an unhealthy situation in a number of ways. White families holding black families in bondage was wrong. The cost of acquiring the number of slaves needed was higher than the cost of the plantation lands and buildings. Owners had so much money invested in their work force that no funds were left for machinery or the development of new ways of cultivation.

In other words, cotton was king, but its reign depended entirely upon slave labor. Other negative factors were present. The South depended on a one-crop economy for a living. Southern leaders had little interest in such civic matters as public education and equal opportunities. The Cotton Kingdom brought a steady widening of social levels so that the rich got richer while the poor got poorer.

Of course, wealthy plantation owners saw nothing wrong with this economic arrangement. As long as cotton harvests were bountiful and profits were high, the South had the strongest voice in national politics and the American economy.

Despite popular belief, only one of every four Southern whites had any direct connection with the slave system. Overwhelming numbers in the society of the Old South were small farmers, shopkeepers, laborers, poor whites who scratched out a living on a few acres of land, and

Appalachian Mountain residents who were far from the mainstream of society and liked it that way.

As different as they were, however, those people had one thing in common that bound them together: the whiteness of their skin. To them, the blacks were simply an inferior race of beings, incapable of living on white civilization's level.

Slavery was an evil, but so many blacks were involved that Southerners viewed the system as a necessary evil for their way of life. The South's population in 1860 was nine million people. Of that number, three and a half million residents (more than one-third of the total) were slaves. In many counties of the Deep South, blacks greatly outnumbered whites. This made "keeping blacks under control" a constant concern.

What slave life was like on a plantation depended on whose views you accepted. In the long years of debate over slavery, the opponents as well as the defenders came forth with equally strong arguments to condemn or support the South's treatment of blacks.

Defenders used arguments from history, economics, and religion. Slavery was as old as man, Southern writers stated. From earliest times, men were in bondage to something: misfortune, crime, war, economic needs. Progress began when captives in battle were put to work rather than put to death. History also showed, defenders of slavery added, that those periods of old in which slavery was most prominent were the very ages that witnessed the greatest achievements of mankind.

Southerners maintained that they did not turn blacks into slaves; blacks were already slaves to the wild jungles of Africa before they were brought to this country. Once in America, people said, blacks could become part of advanced Western culture. They could benefit from all its blessings, including Christianity. A "savage" converted into a slave gained economic value for the first time. He became worth something to somebody other than his family.

Slaveholders gave other reasons in defending what they called the "peculiar institution." Plantation slaves, they claimed, did not have to worry about slack times or lack of jobs, as did the "hired hands" of the North. Black laborers were fed, housed, and clothed, the slaveholders pointed out, and cared for from the cradle to the grave. Their wives and children received the same kind treatment.

On many farms and plantations, the slaves did not even perform hard

Several generations of South Carolina slaves posed for this 1862 photograph.
(Library of Congress)

or dangerous work. The owners had invested too much money in slaves to risk losing them through injury or death.

Another argument put forth by proslavers was both racial and biological. They argued that even adult slaves were children, lacking in intelligence and unable to take care of themselves. Giving them freedom—pushing them into the cold world—would be the cruelest thing that anyone could do. And what would happen to the South if three and a half million workers were suddenly dumped into a society that had no place for blacks to live as the white person's equal?

Without slave labor, Southern businessmen insisted, King Cotton would no longer exist. America might collapse if its principal source of income vanished. Besides, no people had ever been asked to give away two billion dollars in property and receive nothing in return.

Southerners also defended slavery on grounds of inheritance, patriotism, and fellowship. American slavery was almost as old as the American Colonies. Many of the Founding Fathers—including George Washington, "The Father of His Country," and Thomas Jefferson, "The Author of the Declaration of Independence"—had owned slaves. No one had ever accused them of being evil men. Since master and slave spoke the same language, worshiped the same God, and worked the same crops, feelings of love and trust were common on most plantations—the owners said.

As a final point, slaveholders defended their way of life with religious arguments. The Old Testament was full of stories about the "chosen people of God" having bondsmen, bondsmaids, and servants. In the New Testament, Saint Paul had once warned: "Servants, be obedient to them that are your masters. . . ." As for Jesus, Southerners merely pointed out that not once during Christ's earthly ministry did he ever speak out in clear terms against slavery.

Thousands of Americans, North and South, considered the proslave arguments as real and truthful. Nevertheless, those who opposed slavery could also make a strong case.

God did not intend people to be in bondage. Slavery and freedom were two entirely different things, and America's roots had always been planted in the search for freedom.

A slave was totally at the mercy of his master. The owner could buy him, sell him, tell him when and how much he would work, where he would live, and what he could expect to receive for his efforts. The master performed slave marriages and granted divorces; he was both judge and jury for any misbehavior; the punishment a slave received was a decision that only the master made. Abuse came not from the master but more often from the overseer, or slave driver, who managed work in the fields. While such mistreatment was not the general rule, it happened often enough to give plantation life an evil reputation.

Slave auctions were disgusting sights to all but the cold-hearted buyers. Blacks stood in line to be sold to the highest bidder, sometimes alongside horses and cattle. Humans were poked, jabbed, and examined as if they were animals. Husbands and wives were sometimes sold to different owners; children might be wrenched from mothers' arms to become someone else's property. In truth, black families were rarely separated, but the fact that this heartbreaking practice occurred at all was another curse on the whole institution of slavery.

Flogging was a usual form of slave punishment, because the whip was something that even the most uneducated person could understand and

Southern slaves being sold at a public auction. (Harper's Weekly)

fear. Yet contrary to Northern charges, savage beatings were not common on the plantation. Mistreatment promoted less work, as well as the greater risk of a slave running away. If a slave had to be sold for any reason, his value was much less if he had telltale lash marks on his back. Still, some overseers and a few owners employed such weapons of punishment as the whip and the branding iron.

Masters usually stopped their slaves from being educated. Reading leads to thinking, and thinking can lead to unrest. As a result of such restrictions on learning, nearly 90 percent of the adult slaves in the South at the time of the Civil War could neither read nor write.

Slavery, its critics further charged, stripped black people of all pride and dignity. It was a denial of liberty and equality under the natural laws of man. A slave could not have the sense of pride that comes with owning one's home, caring for oneself, and finding work of one's own choice.

Southern ministers who defended slavery on religious grounds soon found their best argument blown apart. As Northern clergy were quick to show, Jesus *did* say something against slavery. His entire ministry rested on the single belief in the universal brotherhood of all men.

Slave labor is forced labor and therefore not always efficient. It is true that cotton production was high throughout the first half of the nineteenth century. Yet critics of the plantation system argued that the yield would have been even higher if the laborers had been paid for their work or given good reason for performing better. A slave did only what he was told because he had little to gain by doing more.

One of the best and most sweeping of the criticisms was that slavery was as harmful to Southern whites as it was to the blacks. Slaveowners were blocking man's natural desire for freedom. They were shaming themselves to the same degree that they were holding the blacks "in their place." Years after the Civil War, the distinguished educator Booker T. Washington would make a painful but true observation. A white man cannot hold a black man in a ditch, Washington said, without getting down in the ditch with him.

2

Abolitionists Begin Their Attacks

HISTORIANS CALL the forty-year era from 1820 to 1860 the antebellum period (*antebellum* meaning "before war"). During that time the seeds of distrust and hatred took root. Cotton production was at its highest. The South truly became a section distinct from the rest of America.

At the same time, the Industrial Revolution began in New England and spread steadily to neighboring areas. Towns and villages became manufacturing centers; new cities sprang up where water power could be found; factories replaced fields as the basic source of income in large parts of the North.

More and more people came to feel that the agricultural South and the manufacturing North were going in opposite directions. In doing so, the two sections were creating a real danger to American unity—a danger that grew when the fight to end slavery began and reached full fury.

In all the controversy over cotton and slavery, it is easy to forget that the new nation then was getting bigger and better in many ways. America's size tripled as the frontier moved westward from the Mississippi River until it reached the Pacific Ocean. Population was doubling every ten to fifteen years. Millions of immigrants from Europe flocked to America's shores and made new homesteads all across the continent.

The antebellum period was also an age of reform. The betterment of man, and renewed hope in the dream of a more perfect society, became major issues of the day. A fresh surge of religion known as the Second Great Awakening began in the North and swept through America. Its goal

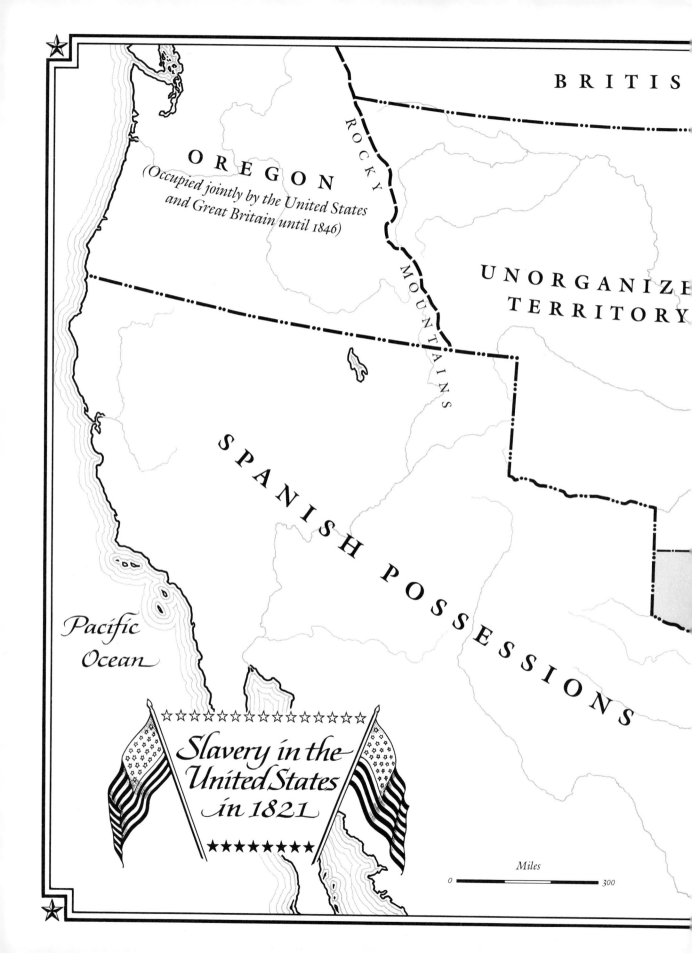

BRITIS

ROCKY

OREGON

(Occupied jointly by the United States and Great Britain until 1846)

UNORGANIZE
TERRITORY

MOUNTAINS

SPANISH POSSESSIONS

Pacific
Ocean

Slavery in the
United States
in 1821

Miles

0   300

OSSESSIONS

N

MAINE

Lake Superior

MICHIGAN
TERRITORY

VERMONT

NEW
HAMPSHIRE

MASSACHUSETTS

Lake Huron

Lake Michigan

NEW YORK

RHODE ISLAND

CONNECTICUT

Lake Ontario

Lake Erie

PENNSYLVANIA

NEW JERSEY

ILLINOIS   INDIANA   OHIO

MARYLAND

DELAWARE

WASHINGTON

MISSOURI

KENTUCKY

VIRGINIA

Atlantic
Ocean

NORTH
CAROLINA

TENNESSEE

KANSAS
TERRITORY

SOUTH
CAROLINA

Mississippi River

MISSISSIPPI   ALABAMA   GEORGIA

Slave-holding
states and territories

LOUISIANA

National capital   ⊙

FLORIDA
TERRITORY

Gulf of Mexico

© 1992 by A. Karl/J. Kemp

was to end all of the sins of humankind. This desire to improve life on earth led to the start of a whole series of reform movements. Better and higher public education, cleaner jails, more attention to the mentally ill, fairer treatment of workers, efforts to end all wars, efforts to stop the use of alcohol, the start of the women's rights movement—all received attention and became part of a great social crusade.

It was natural that a movement to abolish slavery would be part of the Great Awakening. World opinion was shifting in that direction at the time. In the first half of the nineteenth century, Old World countries such as England, France, and Denmark had ended slavery in their colonies. Should not the greatest democracy in the New World do the same at home?

In the beginning, the antislavery campaign in America was a nation-wide effort. Yet as it became more intense, it became a Northern movement. Many Southerners viewed slavery as an evil; but as cotton became king, slavery became a *necessary* evil. To abolish it outright, Southerners tried to explain, would plunge the South into economic and social disaster.

Such arguments made no impression on the militant reformers of that day. To them, keeping human beings in bondage violated the idea of American democracy more than did any other social problem. It was too cruel a system to exist in any way.

The abolition of slavery was never a massive crusade of the entire Northern people. Many Northerners looked with open hostility at the 251,000 freed blacks who lived in their midst. Several Northern states even forbade blacks from living inside their boundaries. The majority of white residents outside the South had few opinions about slavery and chose to ignore it.

In fact, throughout the 1820s the largest group of reformers concerned about the "peculiar institution" did not insist that it be erased. They merely opposed its spreading from the South to other sections of the country. These groups were first known as antislaveryites and later as Free-Soilers.

Stronger in feeling than the antislaveryites in the early part of the antebellum period were the abolitionists. They wanted an end to slavery, but in the beginning they were willing to listen to all proposals about how the system could be abolished. These early abolitionists believed in the need to move calmly and carefully so that the evil of slavery would disappear slowly with as little trouble as possible.

The atmosphere of calm pressure by Northern reformers exploded in 1831 with the appearance of William Lloyd Garrison. Behind the spectacles and mild looks of this twenty-six-year-old reformer was a steel-like determination to see slavery erased at once. Garrison was a natural agitator; he had led several reform movements before he turned his complete attention to slavery. Although Garrison had never seen the slave system in action, he became convinced that it was a curse on America. Those who practiced slavery were criminals, he announced. The whole system must be wiped out by any means.

Using his Boston-based newspaper, *The Liberator,* as a starting point, Garrison soon had a small but hardworking team behind him. They were mostly white, neither wealthy nor poor, and deeply religious. Some of them held positions of influence.

The Garrisonians never listened to reason. They burned copies of the U.S. Constitution because it gave certain protection to slaveholders and was therefore a wicked document. They would not vote in national elections in the belief that any government permitting slavery to exist was itself evil. Many abolitionists wanted the Northern states to leave the Union in order to be free of the sinful South.

Garrison and his followers spent the next thirty years not just attacking slavery in every possible manner but also attacking the slaveholders. Garrisonians spread rumors about slaves everywhere being beaten and tortured. They lied about the overall treatment of blacks in the South.

These strong-minded abolitionists published hymnbooks with new verses striking at slavery in the name of God; they made speeches throughout the country; they sent demand after demand to Congress for laws against slav-

William Lloyd Garrison lashed out at slavery as "a covenant with death and an agreement with hell." (Library of Congress)

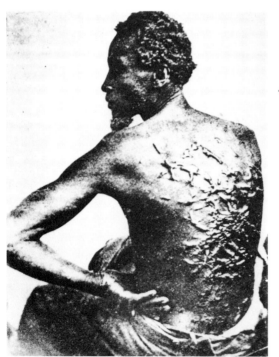

By 1840, Northern newspapers and magazines were publishing drawings of slave whippings in the South (ABOVE). Slaveowners denied such conduct, but this photograph of a badly beaten slave (LEFT) proved that the charges were often true. (Harper's Weekly, above; The Granger Collection, left)

ery; they published newspapers, magazines, sermons, and pamphlets underlining the evil of everything connected with slavery.

Fervent abolitionists reached out to little children as well as grown people. One of their schoolbooks taught the alphabet with poetry. Some of the verses were:

> *I* is the Infant, from the arms
> Of its fond mother torn,
> And at a public auction sold
> With horses, cows, and corn.

> *Z* is a Zealous man, sincere,
> Faithful, and just, and true;
> An earnest pleader for the slave—
> Will you not be so too?

In 1833, Garrison's band joined forces with other abolitionist groups and formed a militant new organization called the American Anti-Slavery Society. The abolitionists then stepped up their verbal war. They called slaveholders "barbarians," "sinners," and "un-American." The last charge stung badly, for Southerners took deep pride in being among the first American settlers.

The antislavery campaign was often ugly. Abolitionists who dared to visit the South were frequently beaten, jailed, or forced to flee for their lives. Mobs in the South tarred and feathered unwanted "troublemakers" and broke into post offices to destroy abolitionist publications waiting to be delivered. A number of Southern state governments passed laws designed to keep slaves under tighter control because of outside pressure.

New laws from Congress and a Supreme Court decision in the 1850s gave Southerners more opportunity to extend slavery farther across the country. The Free-Soilers and moderates willing to accept compromise began to realize that they could no longer keep slavery locked in the South. Hundreds of reasonable people then swung over to the American Anti-Slavery Society. The abolitionists, now with greater numbers, became even louder in their demands.

These fervent crusaders were so outspoken and so daring that Southerners came to think of them as the true voice of the North. This was not so: only one of every twenty Northerners belonged to the abolitionist crusade. Yet this 5 percent of the Northern population did far more in the long run than their small numbers might lead one to believe.

Each year more and more Americans, listening to the abolitionists, became convinced that slavery was a danger to *all* American freedoms. The abolitionists organized political parties and ran for national offices. By keeping slavery the key issue for many years, they made sure that life in America would never be quite the same again.

Southerners could do little more than defend their way of life even more strongly in the face of abolitionist attacks. Hence, slavery became more deeply rooted in the South than ever before. The passing years saw abolitionists and slaveholders steadily form into two angry camps. Each refused to back down; each increasingly accused the other of lies and treason. In that setting, the foundations of the young nation—compromise, democracy, and cool reasoning—began to fade away.

Many Southern slaves fled north to freedom on the Underground Railroad—sympathetic whites and blacks who hid slaves all along their escape route. One of the chief organizers of the system was Harriet Tubman (FAR LEFT), *shown here with a group of runaways she assisted. (The Bettmann Archive)*

3

The Road to War

CIVIL WARS do not usually begin in the same way as do conflicts between two nations. The causes behind most wars—such as disputes over borders or the aggressive acts of one people against another—are not even present when a country fights itself. In a civil war, the two sides live in the same area; they speak the same language; they have the same political habits; they share a common past.

Because of these factors, a civil war does not explode suddenly and with little warning. It comes slowly from a long series of arguments and irritations. Each crisis builds upon the anger caused by the others. The last spark—the final break—may seem minor by itself. Yet by that time the two sides have gone from talking to shouting. It is then a small step from shouting to shooting.

The American Civil War followed this pattern. By the late 1840s, North and South were in a debate that was growing more intense. The events of the next ten years created more and more heat, until finally America plunged into the fires of the bloodiest war it has ever known. The road to that war is easy to follow.

Victory in the Mexican War of 1846–1848 had made the areas of Texas, California, and all the land in between part of the United States. By that time fields in the South were wearing out from the constant planting of cotton. Slaveholders saw in the vast new region a place for the necessary expansion of cotton, as well as of slavery. Northern political leaders who had opposed the war with Mexico were just as determined that the new southwestern empire be free from slavery.

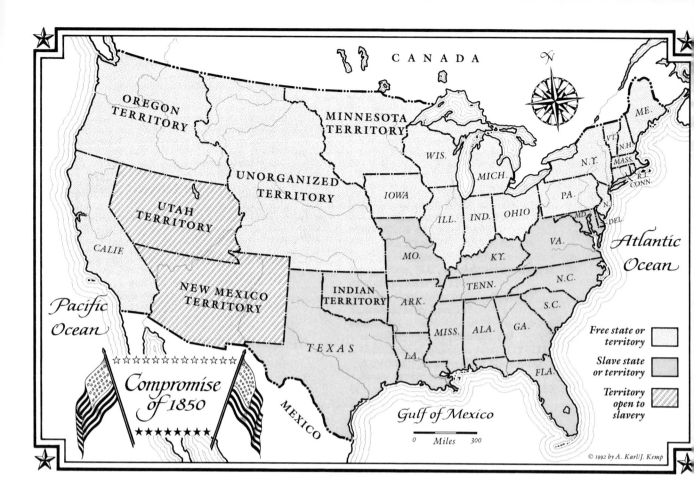

Compromise of 1850

Free state or territory

Slave state or territory

Territory open to slavery

© 1992 by A. Karl/J. Kemp

In 1849, there were fifteen Northern and fifteen Southern states. This gave each side thirty voices in the U.S. Senate, in spite of the fact that far more Americans lived in the North. When the territory of California applied for admission to the Union in 1849 as a free state—a state where slavery would not be permitted—a political battle began. It might have become worse had it not been for Henry Clay, a powerful senator from Kentucky.

Clay sought to calm the troubled political waters by introducing a bill known as the Compromise of 1850. The measure would allow California to become a free state; the rest of the southwestern lands gained in the war would be settled on the basis of popular sovereignty.

Popular sovereignty was a political principle which stated that the people of each new territory would decide whether they wanted to be a free state or a slave state. Such a choice seemed to fit perfectly with the long-held American belief in self-determination—local governance and the right of people to determine the future of their own communities and states. Clay's bill passed and brought an uneasy peace.

Barely a year later, Harriet Beecher Stowe, a Northern writer from a prominent abolitionist family, published a novel entitled *Uncle Tom's Cabin*. The book told a heart-tugging story of the mistreatment of Southern slaves, especially a kindly black man named Tom who was murdered in cold blood by the overseer of a plantation. Southerners dismissed the book as lies from beginning to end. Northerners unfamiliar with slavery came to view this work of fiction as a statement of fact. To them, cruel overseer Simon Legree was a real person. He became, in Northern eyes, the typical Southern white man involved with slavery.

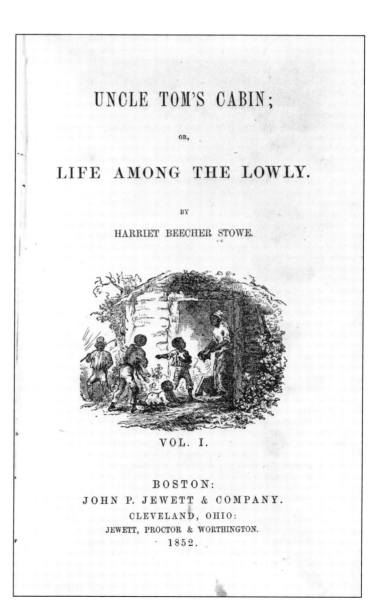

ABOVE: *Harriet Beecher Stowe. (Metropolitan Museum of Art, Gift of I.N.P. Stokes)*
RIGHT: *The title page from* Uncle Tom's Cabin. *The book sold three million copies in the United States and three and a half million copies in other parts of the world. (Library of Congress)*

The 1852 presidential election did nothing to ease tensions. Democrat Franklin Pierce won the election, but he lacked the strength to lead the nation through the gathering storm.

Throughout the early 1850s, as the American frontier continued to move westward from the Mississippi River, more and more people saw the need for a railroad that would connect the nation from the Atlantic to the Pacific oceans. Such a railroad would be of great economic value; it would also bind together isolated communities stretching over a 3,000-mile-wide area into a stronger, single nation.

It soon became apparent that the best route for this transcontinental line would be westward out of the Southern states. The land between Louisiana and California was fairly well settled and protected from bandits, unfriendly Indians, and Mexicans by several army forts. In addition, the railroad would pass through the great Rocky Mountains at their lowest and most narrow points. However, one powerful man disagreed with this plan.

Senator Stephen A. Douglas wanted the railroad to begin at Chicago in his home state of Illinois. The line would then go west to California across the Great Plains and through Colorado. Toward that end, Douglas drafted a bill called the Kansas-Nebraska Act and introduced it in Congress in 1854. The act called for the creation of two huge new territories lying between the Mississippi River and the Rocky Mountains.

Douglas was convinced that the new territories would attract thousands of settlers, who in turn would push the great tribes of Indians aside. Settlers, also called homesteaders, would build towns and communities all over the plains. This would give the North a good chance of becoming the kickoff point for the railroad. Douglas's bill would allow the territories of Kansas and Nebraska to enter the Union and decide for themselves whether to permit slavery or not. This again was popular sovereignty in practice.

Before Douglas could bring his bill forward, he found it necessary to shove another bill out of the way. For thirty-three years the Missouri Compromise had blocked the extension of slavery above the latitudinal line of 36° 30′. All of the proposed Kansas-Nebraska land lay in that no-slave area. Douglas got around this restriction by including in his act a statement removing the Missouri Compromise from the law books.

Abolitionists and Free-Soilers were furious. Douglas was destroying the greatest safeguard the country had against the spread of slavery. South-

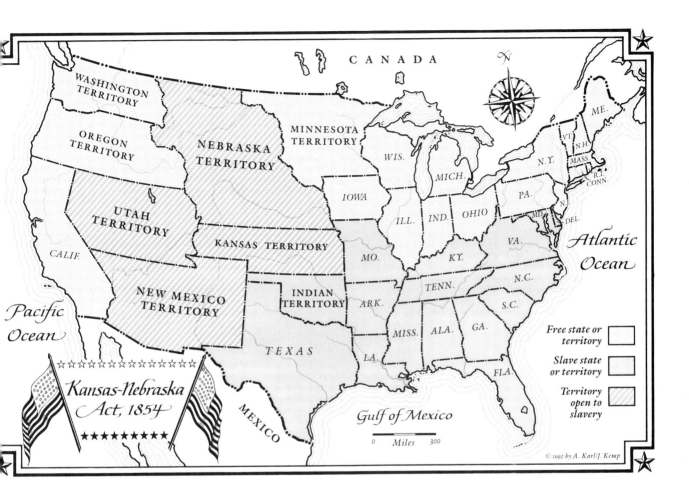

CANADA

WASHINGTON TERRITORY

OREGON TERRITORY

MINNESOTA TERRITORY

WIS.

NEBRASKA TERRITORY

MICH.

N.Y.

ME.

VT.

N.H.

MASS.

R.I.

CONN.

IOWA

PA.

UTAH TERRITORY

ILL. IND. OHIO

N.J.

MD.

DEL.

CALIF.

KANSAS TERRITORY

MO.

VA.

Atlantic Ocean

KY.

Pacific Ocean

NEW MEXICO TERRITORY

INDIAN TERRITORY

ARK.

TENN.

N.C.

S.C.

TEXAS

MISS. ALA. GA.

LA.

FLA.

Kansas-Nebraska Act, 1854

MEXICO

Gulf of Mexico

0   *Miles*   300

Free state or territory

Slave state or territory

Territory open to slavery

© 1992 by A. Karl/J. Kemp

Stephen A. Douglas, the most powerful U.S. senator in the 1850s. (Library of Congress)

erners saw in Douglas's bill a chance to gain still more land for the spread of cotton, plantation society—and slavery.

The Kansas-Nebraska Act became law by a narrow margin of votes. Affairs in America were never the same after that. Reasonable discussion between North and South ended.

Democrats were the only major political party left after the 1852 presidential election. A new faction, known as Republicans, now emerged, largely because of the slavery controversy. Solidly opposed to any further expansion of slavery, the Republicans became a strong political power almost overnight—with roots only in the North. The end of the Missouri Compromise left the Free-Soilers with no place to go except into the ranks of the more fiery abolitionists. The Kansas-Nebraska Act also led directly to bloodshed.

Proslavery elements from the South moved naturally and quickly to settle in nearby Kansas Territory. They were not alone: large bands of abolitionists from the Northern states rushed into Kansas to block the spread of slavery. Determination and dedication collided head-on as two sides waged a bitter contest for one area. With no government to settle the question and no police to keep the peace, many people took the law into their own hands. Fighting became widespread and ugly; killings were daily events. For the next four years, war raged in a region that became known as "Bleeding Kansas."

Violence also spread to the halls of Congress. In the spring of 1856, Senator Charles Sumner of Massachusetts delivered a long speech in which he blamed the South for every evil in the land. South Carolina congressman Preston Brooks responded by beating Sumner severely with a cane in the Senate chamber. A few months later, a free-for-all broke out in the House of Representatives as dozens of congressmen lost their tempers and resorted to fists in an effort to settle their differences.

A new president, the weak and unsure James Buchanan, took office in 1857. He proved to be of no help in the crisis. Indeed, Buchanan had not even unpacked his bags in the White House when, on March 6, 1857, the U.S. Supreme Court dropped a judicial bomb into the sectional bonfire. The case in question involved whether a slave named Dred Scott was entitled to his freedom because he had lived for several years in the free lands of the North.

No, said the Court in strong terms. A slave is private property. The

U.S. Constitution protects the owner's right to a slave, just as it protects the owner's right to his horse, home, and the like. The Court stated further that a slave can be taken anywhere in the country without his status as a slave changing, and that no law can be legal that places any kind of limit on where a slave may or may not go.

Hence, the justices ruled, the Missouri Compromise had always been unconstitutional because no government—not even the Congress—can put up roadblocks to what a person can do with what is lawfully his. The Dred Scott decision also made it clear that the people of a territory do not have the legal power to block slavery when they create a new state. Popular sovereignty, or the right of self-determination in this instance, was illegal.

Abolitionists screamed with rage and swore to continue their crusades in spite of the Supreme Court's views. Southerners became just as angry. Northerners now seemed to be unwilling to obey the laws of the land. Both sides refused to yield, issued warnings, and prepared to take any action necessary against the other. In that environment, only a spark was needed to ignite an explosion.

It came in October 1859 in the person of John Brown. A failure in both business and farming, Brown had migrated as a homesteader to Kansas. There he became a fiery apostle for the abolitionist cause.

Brown was responsible for at least five murders in the Kansas Territory, but he went unpunished. By then he had convinced himself that the evil of slavery could be ended only by bloodshed. So he and a small band

John Brown's life had been one failure after another until he adopted the abolitionist cause. (Library of Congress)

of followers sneaked into Harpers Ferry, Virginia, one quiet night and seized the federal arsenal there. This was the first stage in a plan to lead all slaves in the area to freedom after they had rebelled against their masters.

The twenty-two men in Brown's band killed four citizens at Harpers Ferry before a group of U.S. Marines under the temporary command of army colonel Robert E. Lee arrived from Washington. Troops stormed the small engine house where Brown and his men had barricaded themselves. Two of Brown's sons were among those killed in the brief fight. Brown himself was wounded and taken prisoner. A Virginia court condemned him to death for the crimes of murder and treason. Early in December, Brown was hanged near Charlestown, Virginia.

In the North, thousands of people hailed Brown as a martyr—a man who had freely given his life in a glorious cause. Southerners saw Brown as nothing more than an insane murderer who got what he deserved. Brown's raid on Harpers Ferry was the first real abolitionist invasion of the South. How many more John Browns were there in the North? Southerners asked. Not knowing the answer but fearing the worst, communities all over the South began organizing companies of soldiers for a possible fight.

That was the national mood when the 1860 presidential election took place. The proud old Democratic party could not agree on a candidate. Democrats split into three different groups, each one nominating a man for the presidency.

The new Republican party lost little time in selecting Illinois lawyer Abraham Lincoln as its nominee. Abolitionists filled the Republicans' ranks, and they benefited greatly from the collapse of the Democratic party and the large number of voters in the densely populated Northern states. Lincoln won the election, even though he got only 40 percent of the total vote among the four national candidates.

The election of a president from a political party whose leaders seemed pledged to end slavery was a development that the South simply could not accept. A new life outside the Union began to seem better.

On December 20, 1860, South Carolina passed an "ordinance of secession" that announced its separation from the United States of America. Six other states left the Union within the next two months.

In February 1861, delegates from these states met at Montgomery, Alabama. They organized their own government under the name Confederate States of America. They chose Jefferson Davis of Mississippi as president and Alexander H. Stephens of Georgia as vice president.

Abraham Lincoln and his new government refused to accept the idea of a Southern Confederacy. No state had the right to leave the Union whenever it pleased, Lincoln believed. Any state or combination of states that did so was in rebellion against legal authority. The Lincoln administration would not meet with Confederate officials, and it refused Southern demands that the federal government abandon forts and arsenals inside the Confederate States.

Militia and home guard units in communities throughout the South began seizing federal posts inside the Confederacy. Many Union garrisons laid down their arms without a fight. Federal troops at Fort Sumter, in the harbor of Charleston, South Carolina, refused to surrender. South Carolina officials were determined to seize the brick structure at any cost.

Confederate authorities agreed with their member state and mounted cannon along the beaches on three sides of Fort Sumter. Still the Federal commander refused to yield. On April 12, Confederate batteries opened

Fort Sumter was reduced to a shapeless mass of bricks, wood, and metal. (Library of Congress)

Three-gun battery inside Fort Sumter. (Private collection)

fire on Sumter. The one-sided bombardment lasted thirty-six hours before the small Union garrison lowered its flag in defeat.

The attack on Fort Sumter was a clear act of war. President Lincoln promptly issued a call on all the states for 75,000 volunteers to serve as soldiers in punishing the Southern rebels.

The calling for troops to invade the South forced the states of the upper South to choose between respect for the Union and longtime ties with the South. Virginia, Arkansas, North Carolina, and Tennessee seceded, or left the Union, and joined their sister states. By February 1861, six other states had left the Union—Mississippi, Florida, Alabama, Georgia, Louisiana, and Texas. Kentucky declared itself neutral in the contest. Maryland and Missouri remained in the Union because of strong national feelings plus the presence of Federal troops inside their borders.

The die was cast. North and South had formed sides. Compromise had vanished; war had taken its place. Now it was up to soldiers to decide by force what was to become of the American nation.

One War with Many Names

The confusion of a nation at war with itself still lives in the many titles given to the 1861–1865 conflict.

"Civil War" is the most popular name. Both North and South used the term during the war years. Many Southerners object to "Civil War" because, they say, the title gives the false picture of two sides fighting for control of a single government. It is true that political and military contests were waged early in the war for control of state governments in Tennessee, Missouri, and Kentucky. However, the Confederate States of America wanted to leave the Union, not take control of it. On the other hand, many leading Southerners, including Robert E. Lee, used the term freely.

"War Between the States" became a favorite Southern name in the years after the conflict. The title is confusing because it gives the impression that the rights of the states rather than the expansion of slavery was the major issue in the conflict.

"War of the Rebellion" appeared shortly after the struggle began. Northerners considered the South's withdrawal from the Union to be a rebellion. Two things help to make the term well known. Confederates took pride in being called rebels; and after the war, when all of the battle reports, letters, dispatches, and casualty figures were collected and printed in 128 large volumes, the federal government entitled the collection *The War of the Rebellion: A Compilation of the Official Records of the Union and Confederate Armies.*

"War for Southern Independence" and "Second American Revolution" are among other Southern terms. They attempt to show that Confederates in 1861 were in the same kind of fight for freedom as the colonists were in 1776.

Other names given to the North-South struggle include "The War for Nationality," "War of Secession," "The War Against Slavery," "War of Separation," "Conflict of the Sixties," "The War for the Union," "The Confederate War" (a favorite title of foreign writers), "Mr. Lincoln's War," "The Uncivil War," "The Brothers' War," "War Against the States," "The Lost Cause," and simply "The War."

Some titles hardly give a true picture of the conflict. In this group are "The Yankee Invasion," "The Southern Defense Against Northern Aggression," and "The Late Unpleasantness."

With the passing years, the tendency has been to call the struggle by its simplest title: the Civil War.

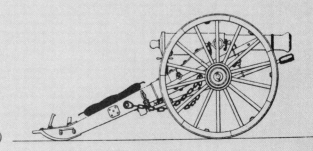

*Field carriage.
(Private collection)*

4

Union vs. Confederate Resources

FEW COUNTRIES have ever been less ready for war than America in the spring of 1861. Aged General Winfield Scott, who had been general in chief of the U.S. Army since 1841, grumbled that Washington, D.C., could have been seized "with a bottle of whiskey."

The tiny prewar army numbered only 16,000 men. It was spread out in 140 forts and outposts stretching over three million square miles, from ocean to ocean. At that time the army could not keep Indians in the West under control. It could hardly be expected to bring one third of the states back into the Union.

Even worse, the U.S. Army was old-fashioned and outmoded. Eight of the nine highest-ranking officers were veterans of the War of 1812, fought a half-century earlier. The War Department was a small, second-rate agency. No general staff existed to attend to the important little details of fighting a war. There were not even accurate maps. One general left for war in 1861 with charts he bought at a local bookstore. The key word to describe the army was *disorganized*.

The North had the advantage of a number of established things: a Congress, the White House, permanent records, a beloved flag, a seventy-year-old Treasury Department, State Department, judicial system, postal service, and the like. However, many officials had left or were leaving to join their Southern states; Republicans led the government for the first time; the defenses of the capital at Washington, D.C., were as weak as they had been back in the War of 1812. No president ever began his duties with more problems waiting for him than did Abraham Lincoln.

Across the Potomac River separating Maryland and Virginia—and North from South—the new Confederate States of America faced even greater difficulties. Southern leaders had to set in motion all the machinery of government, from the approval of a constitution to the creation of dozens of new agencies and bureaus. The infant Southern nation rested on the belief in states' rights—that each state had powers equal to those of the national president and Congress. How to secure the cooperation of all the states in a single war effort was a vital issue.

Equally important, the Confederacy had to raise armies. Unlike the North, the Southern nation had no prewar army on which to build its

A bird's-eye drawing of Washington in 1861, looking southwest. Note the unfinished dome of the U.S. Capitol. In the background are the Potomac River and the hills of Confederate Virginia. (Harper's Weekly)

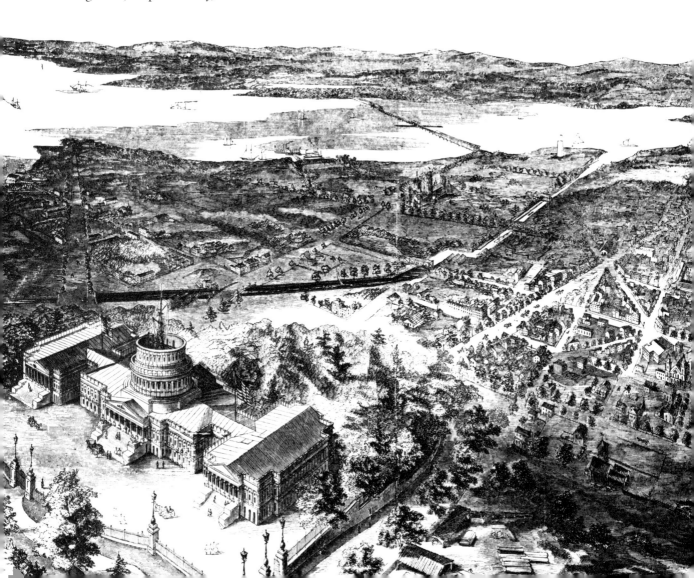

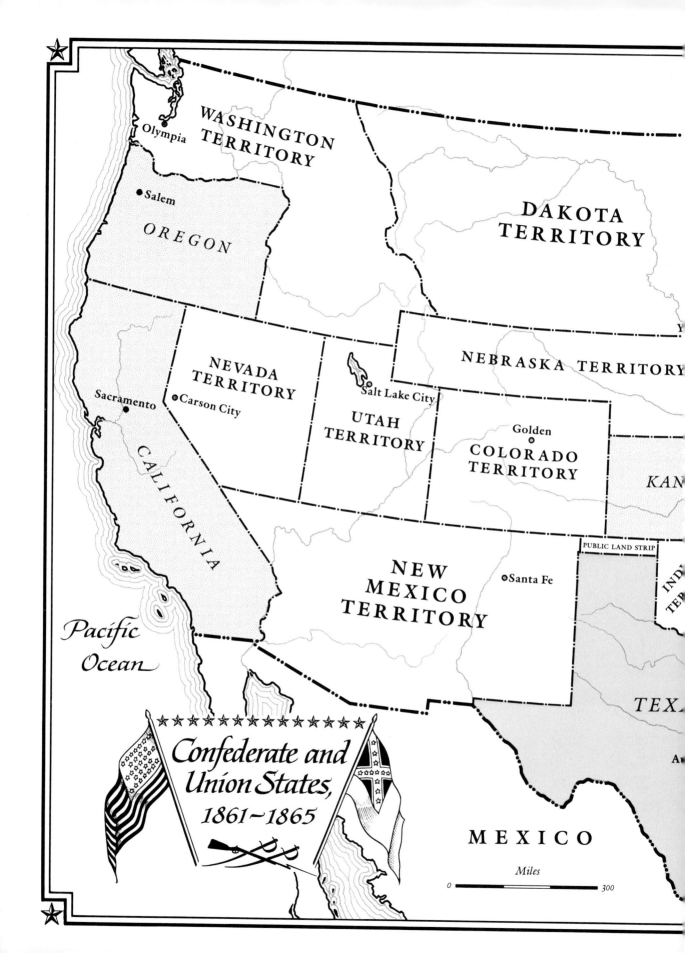

WASHINGTON
TERRITORY

Olympia

●Salem

OREGON

DAKOTA
TERRITORY

NEVADA
TERRITORY

Sacramento●

●Carson City

Salt Lake City

NEBRASKA TERRITORY

Y

UTAH
TERRITORY

Golden
○

COLORADO
TERRITORY

CALIFORNIA

KAN

PUBLIC LAND STRIP

NEW
MEXICO
TERRITORY

○Santa Fe

IND
TER

Pacific
Ocean

TEX

A

Confederate and
Union States,
1861~1865

MEXICO

Miles

0   300

CANADA

MAINE
Augusta

MINNESOTA

Lake Superior

WISCONSIN

Paul

Madison

MICHIGAN

Lansing

Lake Michigan

Lake Huron

IOWA

Des Moines

a City

ILLINOIS

INDIANA

Springfield

Indianapolis

OHIO

Columbus

Lake Erie

Lake Ontario

VERMONT

NEW HAMPSHIRE

Montpelier

Concord

NEW YORK

Albany

Boston

MASSACHUSETTS

Hartford

Providence

CONNECTICUT

RHODE ISLAND

PENNSYLVANIA

Trenton

NEW JERSEY

Harrisburg

MARYLAND

Annapolis

Dover

DELAWARE

ka

Jefferson City

MISSOURI

Frankfort

KENTUCKY

WEST VIRGINIA*

WASHINGTON

Charleston

RICHMOND

VIRGINIA

Atlantic Ocean

ARKANSAS

Nashville

TENNESSEE

Mississippi River

Raleigh

NORTH CAROLINA

Little Rock

MISSISSIPPI

Jackson

ALABAMA

Montgomery

Atlanta

GEORGIA

Columbia

SOUTH CAROLINA

Union states

Confederate states

National capital ◉

Territorial capital ◎

State capital ●

LOUISIANA

Baton Rouge

Tallahassee

FLORIDA

Gulf of Mexico

Territorial boundaries are as of 1861.

*West Virginia became a Union state in 1863.

© 1992 by A. Karl/J. Kemp

fighting forces. Militia companies and home guard units would have to be increased, organized, and molded into armies as quickly as possible.

Some historians believe that Confederate officials made a major mistake in the Civil War's first weeks by moving the South's capital from Montgomery, Alabama, to Richmond, Virginia. Such a transfer, the argument goes, shifted the seat of government from a location deep in the South to a point barely one hundred miles from Washington itself. Yet the reasons for the move far outweigh the factors against it.

Richmond was the principal city in the richest and most populated of the Confederate States. It was also the third-largest city in the South, and it was the nearest thing the Confederacy had to a manufacturing center. Five railroads converged there; a 195-mile canal for inland shipping extended westward into the mountains. Richmond contained the South's largest ironworks, one of the largest arsenals, and many important factories and machine shops. The city had to be protected at all costs.

In the spring of 1861, Southern political leaders felt that their capital

In May 1861, the Confederacy moved its capital from Montgomery, Alabama, to Richmond, Virginia (BELOW). *(Harper's Weekly)*

should be nearer the upper Southern states, where heavy fighting might occur. A tragic result of moving the capital was that it also made the one hundred miles of Virginia between Richmond and Washington the main battle area of the Civil War.

The best way to compare the Northern and Southern nations in 1861 is to look at them under various headings. At first glance, the South appeared too weak to make the approaching conflict any kind of contest. Twenty-three Northern states, with their fields and factories, their bustling seaports and growing cities, stood against eleven farming states in the South.

Manpower. Men for the armies are a nation's most important resource in fighting a war. In the North were 22,000,000 citizens. In the South were 9,000,000 people—but this figure is misleading, for 3,500,000 of those Southerners were slaves whom white authorities were unwilling to consider as potential soldiers.

Hence, 22,000,000 Northerners were at war with 5,500,000 Southern whites. About 2,100,000 Northern men joined the armies. The Confederacy managed to put 800,000 of its men into the field. The Union thus had an almost three-to-one advantage in numbers for battle.

The need for so many Southern men to enter the army led to a crisis on the Confederate homefront. A lack of workers on farms, in mines and foundries, and at other necessary tasks behind the lines caused a breakdown in production. Confederate soldiers suffered throughout the war from a lack of food and supplies.

Several other factors, however, reduced the three-to-one advantage of the North. First, the South had better military leaders in the beginning. Most of the leading military schools of that day, such as the Virginia Military Institute (VMI), The Citadel at Charleston, South Carolina, and the Louisiana Military Academy at Baton Rouge, were in the South. Many of their graduates, along with Southerners who had been educated at West Point, had made the army a lifetime career.

For example, when the Civil War began, such Southern-born officers as Robert Edward Lee, Thomas Jonathan ("Stonewall") Jackson, and Joseph Eggleston Johnston were on active duty or associated with the military. Three former army officers who became well-known Union generals stand in contrast. In 1861, Ulysses Simpson Grant was working in his father's leather-goods store, George Brinton McClellan was a railroad executive,

Among the first to answer the call for troops were militia units that had been organized before the war. Here a well-dressed regiment parades down an avenue in New York City. (U.S. Army Military History Institute)

and William Tecumseh Sherman was in charge of the streetcar system in St. Louis, Missouri.

Southern plantation life had produced clearly different levels of society. Planters and the sons of planters were the unchallenged leaders of their communities. When the war began, they were the men who raised the companies and regiments. Hundreds of them became the captains and colonels of their units. Less well-to-do farmers, clerks, and members of the lower levels of society followed their leaders as naturally into battle as they had followed them in life before the war. Thus, leadership was stronger, at first, with the Southern forces. Heavy battle losses among Confederate field commanders in 1861–1863 would cause superior military leadership to swing to the Northern side after the first two years of fighting.

Matériel (military supplies). The North was so far ahead of the South in this area that a comparison with the biblical figures David and Goliath cannot begin to give a true picture. In 1860, at least 90 percent of America's industrial strength was in the North. It could boast of 110,000 manufacturing companies, while the South had only 18,000 such plants. On the eve of war, the Southern states together produced 37,000 tons of pig iron. In the North, Pennsylvania alone turned out 580,000 tons of the metal.

Only one foundry in the entire South was capable of manufacturing something as big as a railroad locomotive. But the demand for war goods prevented it from doing so. Foundries all over the North could, and did, turn out railroad engines while producing such other matériel as cannon, rifles, and ironclad ships.

Railroads were the main carriers of goods at that time. The "iron horse" bound the nation together as no other form of communication had done. This is why entire military campaigns were waged in the Civil War for nothing more than the control of a single railroad. The South again was very weak in this area. While the North boasted of 23,000 miles of railroad for delivering supplies to its armies, the South had only 9,000 miles of track. Most of the South's railroads were in Virginia and Tennessee. In time, Union armies would destroy them.

Furthermore, the South had few means by which to pay for the war. Its wealth lay in land and slaves, which were of little value in wartime. Cotton was the South's most important product, but the Northern blockade—in which warships blocked vessels going in and out of Southern ports—stopped most of the trade with Europe. Few banks existed in the Confederacy; ready cash was always in short supply. The Southern nation tried every means of taxation. Yet money was scarce, and its value decreased as the struggle continued. This "galloping inflation" became a Confederate way of life.

One Northerner vividly saw these great differences in matériel between North and South. He was William T. Sherman, who became one of the North's most famous generals. In 1860, Sherman wrote to a Southern friend: "In all history no nation of mere agriculturists ever made successful war against a nation of mechanics. . . . You are bound to fail."

Sherman was correct. In 1861, the Confederate States accepted war with eagerness and determination. They did not realize that the real tools for war—iron, coal, meat, grain, and two-thirds of the white male popu-

Federal troops guarding a refueling stop on a railroad line in northern Virginia. (Library of Congress)

lation of the region—were all in the upper South. The major resources of the Confederacy were close to the Northern border. Once Union armies marched into those areas and occupied great chunks of Virginia, North Carolina, Tennessee, and neighboring states, the Confederacy's strength would fade quickly.

Patriotism. Northerners went to war in great numbers to protect the Union and to defend the democratic ideals on which the United States had been founded. But Southerners in 1861 were not too worried by the odds against them. Seventy-five years earlier, the American colonies had rebelled against England, the mightiest empire on earth, and the Americans had won. Southerners felt that fighting in defense of their land, homes, and families was the noblest form of patriotism and worthy of God's protection. Besides, many of the planters exclaimed, foreign aid would surely come from England, from France, or from some other nation once the world saw how right the South was in its war.

Geography.   In size, the Confederacy was a huge nation. Its 750,000 square miles made it twice as large as the original thirteen colonies. Defeating a country that had 3,000 miles of coastline and ran from northern Virginia to the Mexican border seemed like an impossible task to many Northerners.

The geography of the Southern region gave it an even greater advantage in war. Running northeast to southwest through the Confederacy were the Appalachian Mountains. Their peaks were high, their passes few.

This unbroken chain of mountains divided the South in half and created two major theaters of war. The eastern theater stretched from the eastern face of the Appalachians to the Atlantic Ocean. The western theater began on the west side of the mountains and extended to the Mississippi River. A third, less active theater of operations, the trans-Mississippi, began at the west bank of the great river and included such large areas as Arkansas, Kansas, and Missouri.

To bring the South back into the Union, therefore, Northern armies would have to win victories in not one but three different areas. The eastern theater was the most important area to both sides. In it were the two national capitals. For centuries, military men knew that as a rule a country surrendered when its capital fell to the enemy.

Northern officials were convinced in the beginning that the eastern theater was the easiest to conquer. It proved to be the most difficult. Between the mountains and the ocean in upper Virginia the land was only about 150 miles wide. Most of this rolling country consisted of dense forests wrapped around open fields. An army had to move through it slowly and cautiously. Even worse, between Washington and Richmond, six rivers and many creeks ran west to east. Union armies heading south had to cross each one. Confederate forces made each stream a major line of defense. Some of the Civil War's largest battles occurred along the banks of such Virginia rivers as the Rapidan, Rappahannock, Mattaponi, and North Anna.

Strategic position.   The North's primary military task was to bring the South back into the Union. To do that, Northern armies had to invade the Confederacy. This placed the South on the defensive and gave it a major advantage. Confederate forces did not have to extend their thin lines far as they awaited attack.

More importantly, a basic rule of warfare had long been that it takes three men attacking to overcome one man defending. Compare these figures with the three-to-one superiority in Northern manpower, and the odds against the South were no longer as large as they first seemed.

Southerners would also be fighting on familiar ground. Confederates knew the lay of the land: the obscure roads, unused river crossings, and thick woods that provided hiding places for troops. Northern field commanders also found it difficult to obtain military information from Southern residents in areas through which Union forces moved.

Limits of the war.   Southerners were certain that they had a strong advantage in the kind of conflict the Civil War would be. In the old days, men fought wars in a limited way. Each side wanted to capture the other's capital. An army fought until either it seized the enemy's main city or losses became too high. Then the army backed off to fight again another time.

The Civil War, however, was going to be a new and deadly kind of struggle. It was to become a total war because each side fought for an unlimited goal. The North wanted the Union to come back together; just as strongly the South insisted on its independence. Neither unity nor freedom can be compromised. They exist, or they do not.

Southerners fought much of the Civil War with the belief that all they had to do was play for time and wait for the North to grow tired and quit fighting. This struggle could not end that way. It had to be fought to a bitter, complete, and final end. On the other hand, many Northern and Southern leaders realized something else as one bloody month followed another: the Confederacy might actually win in one of two ways.

It could defeat the North, or it could win by not losing. As long as the Southern government still operated to any degree, as long as one group of Southern soldiers was still fighting, as long as a single Confederate flag still waved defiantly somewhere, the Southern nation was alive. And as long as the Confederacy had life, the Union remained broken. Some five and a half million defiant Southerners occupied a land almost the size of Europe. They were confident that while they might be defeated in battle, they could never be conquered in war.

5

1861: Fighting Begins

A TENNESSEAN WROTE of that spring of 1861: "I was a mere boy and carried away by boyish enthusiasm. . . . I was tormented by feverish anxiety before I joined my regiment for fear the fighting would be over before I got into it."

Men on both sides rushed to enter the armies. Few of them had any idea of what lay ahead. Lost in the excitement of the moment was the knowledge that hardships, loneliness, sickness, wounds, and death are part of war. Thoughts only of patriotism, heroism, and glory sent thousands of men, young and old, rushing to the enlistment offices.

When a person enlisted, he first became part of a hundred-man company organized in a town or county. A captain and two lieutenants were in command of a company. The government then banded ten companies (all usually from the same general area) into a regiment. These regiments, led by a colonel, were known by number and state—such as the 18th Virginia, 23rd Massachusetts, 106th Pennsylvania, and the like. A regiment was supposed to have 1,000 men. Sickness, desertion, and battle losses quickly cut that figure in half.

Five regiments formed a brigade (supposedly 5,000 soldiers) under the command of a brigadier general. These units generally contained 3,000 to 4,000 men each. Troops went into battle by brigades because of the traditional belief that when a brigade spread out in a fighting line two columns thick, it occupied a position one mile in length. As the size of armies increased, two other levels of command appeared: divisions (three to five brigades each) and corps (three to five divisions each).

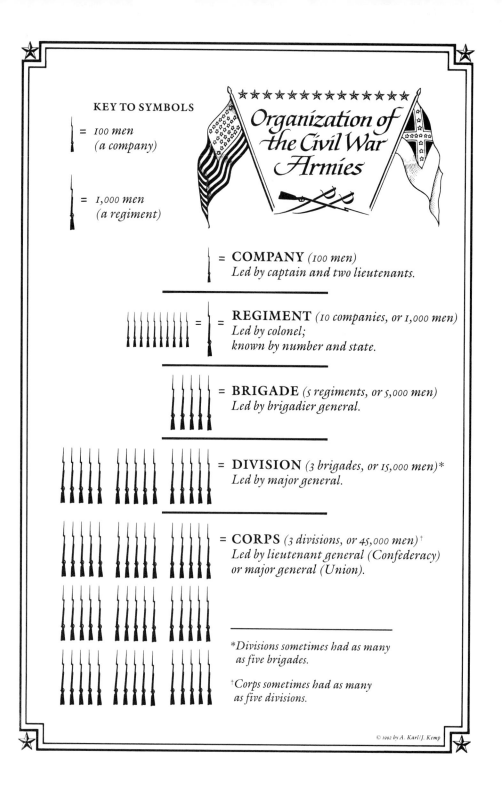

KEY TO SYMBOLS

= 100 men
(a company)

= 1,000 men
(a regiment)

Organization of the Civil War Armies

| = **COMPANY** (100 men)
Led by captain and two lieutenants.

| = **REGIMENT** (10 companies, or 1,000 men)
Led by colonel;
known by number and state.

= **BRIGADE** (5 regiments, or 5,000 men)
Led by brigadier general.

= **DIVISION** (3 brigades, or 15,000 men)*
Led by major general.

= **CORPS** (3 divisions, or 45,000 men)†
Led by lieutenant general (Confederacy)
or major general (Union).

*Divisions sometimes had as many
as five brigades.

†Corps sometimes had as many
as five divisions.

© 1992 by A. Karl/J. Kemp

When banded together, all of these units formed an army. The North usually named armies after rivers. Among the best-known of its huge fighting machines were the Army of the Potomac, Army of the Ohio, and Army of the Cumberland. Confederates used regions as the titles of their armies. The Army of Northern Virginia and the Army of Tennessee were the major Southern forces in the field.

States, towns, and wealthy individuals provided the uniforms early in the Civil War. The result was a confusing collection of styles and colors on both sides. Soldiers wore everything from the French uniform of short blue coat and baggy red trousers to the plain buckskin garb of frontiersmen. Some regiments of Irish-American soldiers dressed in green; other units proudly marched in uniforms of practically every color in the rainbow.

In time, blue became the official Northern uniform color, gray the standard uniform of Confederates. Yet in many of the first engagements, several Northern regiments wore gray and some Confederate units were in blue. This sometimes caused troops to fire into—and kill—their own men.

It took time for the two sides to be ready to fight. However, North and South alike moved quickly to strengthen themselves for war. Only hours after Virginia seceded, state militia units organized before the war seized Harpers Ferry. This village, which John Brown had raided eighteen months earlier, stood on the peninsula where the Shenandoah River empties into the Potomac. Harpers Ferry was the site of a valuable Federal arsenal. It was also the gateway to the Shenandoah Valley, a 160-mile-long farmland whose bountiful fields, flocks, and herds would earn it the name "Breadbasket of the Confederacy."

In the third week of April 1861, Virginia troops occupied the U.S. Navy base near Norfolk. It was the largest shipbuilding facility in the South. The Virginians captured most of the naval machinery, as well as 1,200 cannon, tons of ammunition, and a powerful warship, the USS *Merrimack,* which had been burned to the waterline by the retreating Federals.

To protect Washington and the Union, the federal government also moved swiftly to hold on to the border states of the upper South. Union troops occupied Baltimore and other important points in Maryland. The necessity for this became apparent on April 19, when Baltimore citizens loyal to the South attacked the 6th Massachusetts as that regiment passed through town on its way to the defense of Washington. Maryland would contribute fighting men to both sides, but the state remained under Federal control throughout the war.

Kentucky was the key border state in the western military theater. It

Harper's Ferry, in what is now West Virginia, stands at the junction of the Potomac and Shenandoah rivers. (Harper's Weekly)

was the most divided of all states in sentiment. Shortly after becoming president, Lincoln exclaimed: "I hope God is on our side, but I *must* have Kentucky." State officials struggled constantly to keep Kentucky neutral. But it could not avoid war and became the scene of a number of military activities. Some 50,000 Kentuckians served in the Union armies, while 35,000 others joined the Confederate forces.

The first engagements of the Civil War were collisions between armed mobs rather than battles between trained armies. Neither side was prepared to fight by early summer. Public pressure mounted to wage the one major battle that supposedly would end this sectional crisis. That struggle occurred on July 21 in the eastern theater, and only thirty miles from Washington.

Federal general Irvin McDowell was a dedicated soldier. He had been jumped three ranks from major to brigadier general just that spring. McDowell had never led so much as a company in battle. Worst of all, the "main Union army" that he commanded was, in fact, nothing more than 25,000 green recruits who had rushed from all over the North to defend

Washington. McDowell knew that his troops were not ready to fight. But he obeyed Lincoln's orders and led his regiments south from the Federal capital to do battle.

To protect Washington against Confederate assault from the south or west, McDowell first had to march two days into the central part of Virginia, known as the Piedmont, and capture Manassas Junction. There a railroad from the Shenandoah Valley united with the main line going south from Washington. Confederate general Pierre Gustave Toutant Beauregard, a dashing and self-confident officer, expected McDowell to move on Manassas to secure the important railroads.

Beauregard had no doubts about Federal intentions. Spies in Washington, as well as newspaper reports, kept Beauregard informed of both McDowell's preparations and the strength of his forces.

By mid-July, Beauregard had carefully placed his 20,000 Confederates along the south bank of Bull Run, a quiet stream north of Manassas. Another 12,000 Southern troops were at Winchester in the lower (southern) end of the Shenandoah Valley. They were under the command of experienced General Joseph E. Johnston, a great-nephew of American Revolution hero Patrick Henry.

In front of Johnston stood another Federal army as hastily organized as McDowell's. The sole duty of that second force was to keep Johnston's force in the valley from joining Beauregard. The Federal commander of the army was General Robert Patterson, an aged veteran of the War of

Confederate general Pierre G. T. Beauregard, winning commander at both Fort Sumter and First Manassas. In later campaigns Beauregard was unable to live up to the praise heaped upon him in 1861. (Library of Congress)

A Harper's Weekly drawing of the battle of First Manassas shows Federal troops charging toward Henry House Hill, a piece of high ground that overlooked—and was therefore key to—the whole battle. (Harper's Weekly)

1812. Patterson found himself first confused and then outflanked. Most of Johnston's men joined Beauregard at Manassas on the eve of the battle. Their numbers fairly well balanced the size of the two opposing forces.

Throughout the hot Sunday of July 21, McDowell's green troops hammered repeatedly against the left flank, or side, of the Southern line. They might have broken through had it not been for a Virginia brigadier general and his five regiments posted atop a hill commanding the whole battlefield. That general's name was Thomas J. Jackson. His troops beat back the Union attacks. Their commander was known thereafter as "Stonewall."

Fresh Confederates from the Shenandoah Valley rushed onto the Manassas battlefield in late afternoon. Aided by troops from the other end of the Southern line, they charged into McDowell's attacking columns and sent the Northerners reeling backward. What began as an orderly withdrawal quickly turned into chaotic flight as privates and generals alike ran, loped, and hobbled back toward Washington.

Total losses on both sides at First Manassas (or First Bull Run, as the Federals called the battle) were 868 killed and 2,583 wounded, with an additional 1,011 Federals seized as prisoners of war. This was a small contest by the standards of later Civil War engagements. Still, it had been the largest and bloodiest battle in U.S. history up to that time.

Confederate soldiers and civilians alike celebrated the one-sided victory. The North, shocked by defeat, began building its strength in order to win future battles. Lincoln replaced the unlucky McDowell with an ambitious and self-assured general named George B. McClellan. Only thirty-four years old, McClellan was a good engineer, well read in military matters, and a superb organizer of troops. He seemed to be the right general at the right time for the North, and he soon became general in chief of all Union armies.

Unfortunately, McClellan would come to believe that he alone was the man who could save the Union. He gave little attention to public opinion and even less to his commander in chief, President Lincoln. In the next eight months of 1861–1862, McClellan avoided all military movements as he slowly created his Army of the Potomac, which would ultimately total 150,000 men—the largest single fighting force ever seen outside Europe.

In the western theater, the pitiful thinness of the Confederate defense line became apparent in the first months of war. In September a small Confederate force tried to secure a toehold in Kentucky by occupying the city of Columbus, which overlooked the Mississippi River. Federal forces under General Ulysses S. Grant promptly seized both Paducah and Smithland, Kentucky. These two towns were at the mouths of the Tennessee and Cumberland rivers.

Grant then attacked a Confederate force at Belmont, Missouri, across the river from Columbus. He drove the Confederates out of their camps. The arrival of Southern reinforcements then forced the Federals to retreat to the river transports that had carried them into position at Belmont.

More Federal troops arrived, and the Confederates abandoned the area.

This left Grant in firm control of the lower Ohio River, and it gave the North an ideal "jumping-off" point. Union forces could deliver strikes from the Ohio up the Tennessee and Cumberland rivers into the heart of Tennessee, the Confederacy's western stronghold.

In the third military theater, the trans-Mississippi west of the great river, the fight for control of Missouri began early and became bitter. During April and May, Governor Claiborne Jackson placed the state volunteer troops under Confederate officers and tried to seize the huge St. Louis arsenal with its 60,000 muskets and other munitions. Federal captain Nathaniel Lyon surrounded the volunteers with two companies of infantry (foot soldiers) and forced their surrender. When Federals marched the prisoners through St. Louis, townspeople attacked the soldiers. More than thirty people were killed during two days of fighting.

Lyon received reinforcements as well as a promotion to brigadier general. He then organized a larger Federal force and in mid-June defeated a small Southern detachment at Boonville, Missouri. In August, however, Lyon rashly launched an attack at Wilson's Creek, Missouri.

Many Confederates were wearing blue uniforms that day because gray had not yet become the standard Southern color. This kind of confusion helped the larger Confederate army as it overran one wing of Lyon's army and sent the other scurrying in defeat. Lyon was killed in the thick of the action. Each side suffered 1,300 losses.

The Confederate commander in the area, General Sterling Price, then began an offensive of his own. On September 20, Price's men seized the Federal stronghold at Lexington alongside the Missouri River. Two-thirds of Missouri was now in Confederate hands.

Lyon's successor at the head of the Federal forces was General John Charles Frémont. He issued orders declaring the whole state to be under his military control, and further directed that all slaves of Southern sympathizers were to be freed. He warned Southern irregular troops, called guerrillas and bushwhackers, that they would be executed if captured. Such harsh measures increased bitterness on both sides in Missouri. The state remained in the Union, but it suffered terribly from raids and looting by marauding bands of guerrillas.

As 1861 drew to a close, Virginia became the only state to lose territory as a direct result of the Civil War.

The western third of the state was mountainous. Its people had little farmland and money, and no involvement with the institution of slavery. They were convinced that well-to-do citizens in the tidewater region—the eastern section close to Richmond—dominated Virginia life and did so to the neglect and at the expense of the mountain residents.

When civil war began, North and South recognized the importance of the western Virginia region. Both sides sent troops into the area. The Federals won easy victories in small battles at Rich Mountain and Carrick's Ford. Most of Virginia from the mountains to the west was now under Union control.

The protective presence of Federal troops offered the opportunity that political leaders in the region had wanted. In the autumn of 1861, delegates from fifty western counties banded together and asked the federal government to admit the area into the Union as a new state to be called Kanawha, the Indian name of one of the region's largest rivers. In 1863, the U.S. Congress would approve statehood. This new addition to the Union was given the more meaningful name of West Virginia.

Confederate signal tower.
(Private collection)

How the Rifle Changed War

Americans went to war in 1861 armed with everything from shotguns and blunderbusses to butcher knives and axes. The weapon preferred by most soldiers was the Springfield musket (below, with bayonet). Named for the Massachusetts arsenal where it was manufactured, the Springfield was long (58 inches) and heavy (just under 10 pounds). It was also difficult to use because powder and ball had to be dropped into the barrel and tamped down with a long ramrod, after which a firing cap for exploding the powder was placed at the rear of the barrel. In the heat of battle, the best soldiers could not load and fire more than three shots per minute.

The musket balls of that day were almost three times as large as the bullets used by U.S. troops in the Gulf War. They were of soft lead and the size of toy marbles, and they did not have a pointed shape that would send them smoothly through the air. Although the balls could travel about 250 yards, a soldier could not count on hitting a target more than 80 yards away—less than the length of a football field.

Without question, the most important change in weapons during the Civil War was the development of the rifle. *Rifle* comes from rifling, a process by which gunmakers cut a curving groove along the inside of the smooth musket barrel. Next they took the round musket ball and formed it into a bullet with a pointed end.

When a soldier pulled the trigger, the rear edge of the long bullet spread into the groove, or rifling. This caused the bullet to spin rapidly as it came out of the barrel. As a result, the rifle bullet could travel farther and hit harder.

Now a soldier had the ability to hit an enemy 400 yards away instead of 80 yards. Thus, defenders could fire up to five times more shots at an attacking column than before. In other words, the introduction of the rifle gave the defense a tremendous edge over the offense. Great frontal assaults that had usually carried the day in the past now had to begin farther back from the enemy line because of the rifle's 400-yard range. The charge was longer, subject to heavier fire, and extremely costly as a result.

Field commanders were slow to see this major change. They did not recognize the power of the new rifle. As late as 1864, generals on both sides were still ordering head-on assaults against fortified positions. Such attacks were beaten back with horrible slaughter.

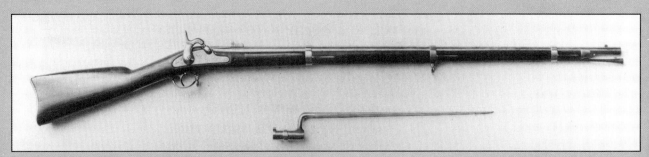

(Smithsonian Institution)

6

Two Presidents and Their Problems

ABRAHAM LINCOLN and Jefferson Davis had much in common. They were fellow Kentuckians, born within one hundred miles of each other. They were only eight months apart in age. Both men were unusually tall and thin. Both read much, thought deeply, and were skilled public speakers. Each was elected president of his nation on the eve of war. Each proved to be a devoted patriot who sincerely loved his country.

In many respects, however, the two leaders were very different. Davis was refined and cultured; Lincoln was a product of western pioneer life. The Southern president had experience in both military and political affairs; the Northern chief executive came into office with limited preparation for the highest seat in government. Davis, who had achieved greater prewar fame, had many social and economic advantages that Lincoln did not.

Davis had every reason to become the better head of state. Yet many Americans today consider Lincoln the greatest of all presidents. Davis appears ineffective, and in some respects a failure.

The reasons for this can be found in the governmental problems they faced, their differing personalities, and the way they acted in the high office they held.

Lincoln was born on February 12, 1809, in a one-room log cabin in the middle of the Kentucky wilderness. His father was an uneducated farmer who soon moved westward, first to Indiana and then to the open-prairie country of Illinois. Abraham Lincoln educated himself. He read any book he could find and knew the Bible well.

In his early years he was a rail splitter, flatboatman, storekeeper, county postmaster, surveyor, and captain of militia. Lincoln then studied law and became a popular attorney in the state capital of Springfield. He served four years in the state legislature. In 1842, Lincoln married Mary Todd, a member of a prominent slaveholding family of Kentucky. The Lincolns had four sons. Two of them died in youth.

By the middle of the 1850s, Lincoln was a familiar and effective politician in Illinois. He could amuse people with homespun stories and thrill them with political speeches. His only experience in national politics had been a single uneventful term in the U.S. Congress.

After joining the new Republican party in 1856, Lincoln rapidly came to the nation's attention. His writings contained a clarity and a compactness rarely seen in any age. Lincoln was also one of the most skillful public speakers of his time. Few could match him in debate, whether in a small courtroom or before a large crowd in some town square.

Every physical part of Lincoln, from his coarse and unruly hair to his huge (size fourteen) feet, seemed unusual. He stood six feet four inches

tall and loomed above everyone around him. Deep hollows and long shadows lined his rugged face. Although Lincoln liked to tell jokes and enjoyed a good laugh, he appeared to most people a tired and unhappy man. An artist who painted his portrait late in the Civil War stated that Lincoln had "the saddest face I ever saw. There were days when I could scarcely look at it without crying."

Lincoln first received national attention in 1858 when he ran against Stephen A. Douglas for the U.S. Senate. Douglas won reelection, but Lincoln's success in a series of debates with Douglas brought him recognition as one who spoke in a style that could be plain, tough, and moving.

In 1860, Lincoln received the Republican nomination and won election as president of the United States. As the sixteenth president, he journeyed to Washington with civil war waiting for him.

Lincoln's extreme height is evident in this photograph, taken when the president visited McClellan (facing Lincoln) in the field in October 1862. (Library of Congress)

For the next four years, Lincoln devoted his energies to winning that war for the Union. He faced endless crises that would have shattered a weaker man. Criticism of him was constant and loud. He had to handle jealous politicians and unsuccessful generals. Almost daily Lincoln was forced to make major decisions on matters that the country had never faced before. He worked at a pace no ordinary person could have maintained. Through it all, Lincoln had to learn how to be a president.

Add to these problems a host of others that Lincoln faced: the heartache over thousands of Union casualties, despair over one military defeat after another in the war's first years, doubts about whether the Union could hold together through the war, and a growing concern over what to do about three and a half million slaves in the South.

In addition to these heavy national problems were personal burdens that Lincoln had to bear: a lack of formal education, a rough appearance, unpolished manners, the loss of his favorite son in the middle of the war, and occasional periods of depression. But Lincoln was courageous, tough when necessary, and deeply patriotic. He considered patience to be his strongest virtue. Even in the worst of times, he displayed coolness. Lincoln endured disappointments from his generals on dozens of occasions. He held his temper in check and exhibited kindness when anger would have been more natural.

Another of Lincoln's well-known qualities was his genuine love of people. He spent hours talking with common folk; he visited army hospitals and greeted soldiers in the front lines. Thousands of Northerners, civilians as well as soldiers, thought of him as a father and called him "Old Abe." In 1863, when Lincoln had to issue a call for 100,000 new troops, the response was so great that a new war song appeared: "We Are Coming, Father Abraham, Three Hundred Thousand Strong."

Religion was a deep and personal matter to Lincoln. He once told a friend: "Without the assistance of that Divine Being, I cannot succeed. With that assistance, I cannot fail." Lincoln quoted often from the Bible, and most of his speeches make reference to God.

Lincoln also had a wonderful sense of humor on which he relied when the burdens of office became heavy. He especially enjoyed laughing at himself. A political enemy once called the homely-looking Lincoln a two-faced man. Lincoln replied: "Now I leave it to my audience. If I had another face, do you think I would wear this one?"

Behind the country-bumpkin appearance, however, was the mind of

No two images reveal the trials and sadness of civil war more than these two photographs of Abraham Lincoln. The picture on the left was taken in 1860; the photo on the right was made only five years later and just days before Lincoln's death. (American Heritage)

one of the most skilled political leaders America has ever known. Lincoln had an extraordinary ability to see people as they were. He paid no attention to braggarts and fired those who did not perform well. On the other hand, when he found capable individuals, he put them to work and gave them all the room they needed to do their job fully.

As a political leader, Lincoln also displayed a marvelous sense of timing. He had the knack of making a certain statement—or removing a certain general from command—at just the right moment. Above all, Lincoln displayed (perhaps better than any American president) what is called a "capacity for growth."

In 1861, not many people felt he had the ability to be a successful president. Yet Lincoln seemed to grow stronger each year. With fierce determination he pursued the ideal that the Union must be preserved at all costs.

To do that, Lincoln often violated the Constitution by going beyond the powers of his office. He shut down several antiwar newspapers and arrested hundreds of Northern citizens whose loyalties were questionable. At times he exercised a number of powers that belonged to Congress, and he ignored that body whenever necessary.

His Emancipation Proclamation granted freedom to all slaves in the Confederacy. The world remembers him for that deed. On the other hand, the proclamation was a presidential order without full legal authority. The document was issued in part to enlist more support from abolitionists and black leaders. By making the end of slavery a major Northern war goal, Lincoln's proclamation blocked England, France, and other nonslaveholding countries in Europe from giving aid to the Confederacy.

Strong presidents must act strongly in time of war. Lincoln's actions frightened many people, but those same actions helped bring victory to the Union.

Lincoln was the first U.S. president murdered while in office. At his death, grief swept across the land to an extent Americans had never known before. Cries for revenge against the Southern leaders might have led to a new and even worse bloodbath. Yet for the moment the North wrapped itself quietly in sorrow. It did so by remembering Lincoln's own words, spoken at his second inauguration only a month before he died: "With malice toward none; with charity for all; with firmness in the right, as God gives us to see the right, let us strive on to finish the work we are in; to bind up the nation's wounds; . . . to do all which may achieve and cherish a just and lasting peace among ourselves, and with all nations."

Lincoln's remains lie today beneath a large stone structure in Springfield, Illinois. His most famous monument is the Lincoln Memorial in Washington, D.C. There a majestic statue of the seated president looks out on the city—and the country—that he gave his life to save.

JEFFERSON DAVIS was also a brilliant public figure. Nevertheless, he was a good man in the wrong place at the worst time. He was thrust into an impossible job: president of a collection of states, each of which insisted on its independence even as members of the Southern Confederacy. Davis gallantly tried to be a leader of all those states, but he found himself battling a human wall of states' rights. Saddest of all, Davis was a dedicated patriot who was never quite able to inspire others with his own soul-deep devotion to the Southern cause.

He was born on June 3, 1808, of fairly well-to-do parents. His father, Samuel Davis, soon migrated from Kentucky to the undeveloped state of Mississippi. There the father became a successful cotton planter and slaveholder. The younger son, Jefferson, received an excellent education, even

Jefferson Davis did not want to be the Confederate president, but he carried out his duties with dignity, courage, and total devotion. (Library of Congress)

by today's standards. He spent two years at a Catholic academy and three years at Transylvania University before entering the U.S. Military Academy at West Point, New York.

Davis graduated from West Point and entered the U.S. Army. He resigned from service after a few years of frontier duty. Increasing the wealth of the family's Mississippi plantation occupied his time until the outbreak of the Mexican War in 1846. Davis took command of a Mississippi regiment, performed valiantly in two major battles in Mexico, received a wound in the foot, and hobbled home to a hero's welcome. The military always remained his first love.

A highly successful political career followed. Davis served two years in the U.S. House of Representatives and eight years in the U.S. Senate. From 1853 to 1857, he was secretary of war during the Franklin Pierce administration. Davis became the best war secretary the nation has ever had. That post, and able service as chairman of the Senate Military Affairs Committee, gave Davis a knowledge of army matters unmatched by any civilian of his day.

Few men of the nineteenth century had read more works on politics and military affairs than Davis. This accomplishment resulted partly from a personal tragedy. His first wife was Knox Taylor, the daughter of General (later President) Zachary Taylor. She died of malaria only three months after marrying Davis.

He barely survived the disease himself. So deep was Davis's sorrow that he shut himself off from the world on his brother's plantation. For seven years, Davis did little but read books, journals, and newspapers.

Davis then married Varina Ann Howell, daughter of a wealthy Mississippi planter. She was eighteen years younger than Davis, but they enjoyed a happy and long life together. Mrs. Davis was a sparkling and charming woman whose intelligence was of valuable help to her husband. Sadly, all four of their sons preceded the parents in death. One of them died during the Civil War when he accidentally fell off the balcony of the presidential mansion in Richmond.

By 1861, Davis was the South's leading statesman. He resigned from

In 1884 Jefferson Davis posed with his family and one of their maids on the porch of their Mississippi home. (Library of Congress)

the Senate and returned home when Mississippi seceded. Davis's dream was to become a Confederate general and lead an army into battle. He was at first disappointed on learning of his election as president of the Southern nation. However, with an unfailing love of his country, Davis accepted his people's call.

This tall, erect, gray-haired leader had many outstanding qualities. Davis was courteous and dignified. A Confederate lieutenant who first saw the president in 1862 wrote of Davis: "He bears the mark of greatness about him beyond all persons I have ever seen. . . . Above all, the gentleman is apparent, the thorough, high-bred, polished gentleman."

Davis did not have Lincoln's gift with words, but then few people do. Yet he was a good speaker. His addresses were always clear and logical. Davis was also honest to a fault. He simply would not bend or compromise on an issue if he felt that he was correct.

Although Davis had received part of his education at a Catholic school, he switched to the Episcopal faith and went regularly to church services. He was a tireless worker who often passed up meals in order to attend to pressing business. Davis also had the moral strength to do the things that seemed right, whether or not public opinion agreed with him. Lastly, Davis's devotion to the Confederate cause was total.

It would be easy to say that Davis failed as a president simply because no man could have brought success to a hodgepodge collection of proud states posing as a nation. Yet Davis proved to be one of his own worst enemies. Flaws in his character appeared early in the war and magnified as the struggle grew more intense.

Davis was a bad administrator in several ways. He was not experienced in giving direction to large numbers of people. At the same time, he often chose the wrong men for jobs and would not leave able assistants alone to do their work. Davis seemed always to think that he could do any task better than the person assigned to it.

Because he was a slow worker fascinated by details, Davis failed to keep pace with the scores of problems that screamed daily for his attention. Cabinet meetings were frequent and often lasted four hours or more as the president wandered from subject to subject. Davis wasted days in writing long letters that a secretary could—and should—have handled.

Despite his long years of public service, Davis did not know how to gain favor with the people. He did not mingle easily in a crowd. To everyone except his family and a small circle of friends, Davis appeared aloof and distant. Even a longtime colleague, Secretary of the Navy Stephen Mallory, admitted that "few men could be more chillingly, freezingly cold" than the Confederate president.

This shortcoming brought Davis into personal conflict with Southern leaders at every level. He quarreled with his vice president, with congressmen, cabinet members, generals, governors, and newspapermen. He fell out with popular figures while clinging with blind loyalty to friends who did not have the confidence of the public.

Davis was impatient and short with anyone who disagreed with him. In fact, he tended to form a strong dislike for individuals who had opinions different from his own. His four years in office witnessed a host of bitter disagreements that hurt the Confederacy as much as they weakened Davis's influence.

The Southern president gave too much time and attention to military matters that should have been left to the secretary of war and the generals in the field. The Confederacy had good commanders who performed well on their own. Unfortunately, Davis was more interested in being a commander in chief than in being a president concerned with social, economic, and political matters behind the lines. Davis neglected areas where he could have been useful and meddled in areas where he was not needed.

Ill health further sapped Davis's effectiveness. He was sick for much of the war period as a result of several ailments: indigestion, boils, pain from a nervous disorder, inability to sleep, and migraine headaches. In 1851, he had lost the use of his left eye. The strain of so much paperwork during the Civil War came close to making Davis totally blind.

Perhaps the greatest of his weaknesses was his failure to grow in office. Davis let the presidency become bigger than he was. He fretted about his problems but refused to compromise; he lost supporters in a steady stream and slowly fell from public favor. Nevertheless, and to the end of the war, he never ceased his efforts on behalf of the land he loved.

Defeat and two years' imprisonment at the hands of the North produced a dramatic turnaround both in Davis's personality and in the feelings of the Southern people.

He returned to the South in 1867 as a hero. In Southern eyes, Davis was a living martyr of those once-glorious days that Confederates proudly remembered as the "Lost Cause." Love and affection that Davis had never known poured upon him from all over the South. He spent his last twenty years making speeches and writing his memoirs while enjoying the people's adoration. He grew old with grace; in 1889, he died with dignity.

As Lincoln pleaded for peace near the end of his life, Davis did the same. A year before his passing, Davis told an audience of young Southerners: "Let me beseech you to lay aside all rancor, all bitter sectional feeling, and to make your places in the ranks of those who will bring about a consummation devoutly to be wished—a reunited country."

Davis is buried in Richmond's Hollywood Cemetery. Also in that city is an imposing monument to the Southern president. It seems so alone, and so distant, from the other memorials in the former Confederate capital.

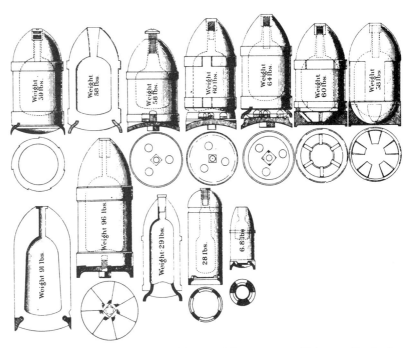

Drawings of rifle projectiles used by Confederate army. (Private collection)

7

1862: The Terrible Hand of War

★ WAR STRUCK IN 1862 with a fury that Americans had never seen before. A young Virginia captain would write that spring: "The whole land which was smiling with plenty and peace has since become a vast arena of deadly strife."

The first great explosion came in Tennessee. In the prewar army, General Albert Sidney Johnston (no relation to Confederate general Joseph E. Johnston) had been one of the highest-ranking and most respected officers. Yet as Confederate commander of the western theater, Johnston found his problems far beyond his—or anyone else's—capacity. He was supposed to defend the entire theater with a 300-mile line stretching from Cumberland Gap on the Virginia border to the Mississippi River. Only 25,000 Southern recruits were available to tackle the job. In trying to defend every point, Johnston's force was too weak to protect any point.

Early in February, following two months of skirmishes, the Federal army began a major advance. Its commander was General U. S. Grant, a short, quiet officer whose plainness concealed a tough, hard fighter. Grant's aim was to gain control of the Tennessee and Cumberland rivers. Those waterways were like broad avenues leading through Tennessee to Alabama and Mississippi.

At a point where the two rivers were only twelve miles apart, Johnston built two earthen fortifications: Fort Henry, on the east bank of the Tennessee, and Fort Donelson, on a bluff along the west bank of the Cumberland. Neither fort had enough men or guns to resist a strong Federal attack.

Grant's plan called for a joint army-navy operation. He loaded his

15,000 infantrymen onto ships. Accompanied by seven gunboats—four of which had been built just for this campaign—the armada steamed up the Tennessee toward Fort Henry. Mother Nature made it easy for the Federals. The Tennessee River was rising rapidly from heavy downpours. The poorly located fort was disappearing under water when, on February 6, the Union gunboats opened fire. Barely a hundred Confederates were inside the fort. They maintained the uneven cannon duel for two hours, then surrendered.

A week later, with his army increased to 27,000 bluecoats, Grant stood ready to attack at Fort Donelson. The Federal gunboats had steamed back down the Tennessee, eastward a few miles up the Ohio River, and then southward again on the Cumberland. Grant's hope was to strike Donelson by land and river at the same time. However, Confederate batteries beat back the gunboats. Johnston had also rushed additional troops to defend the fort. Two days of infantry fighting in bitterly cold weather followed. Thanks more to Confederate mistakes than Federal achievements, the Donelson garrison soon found itself trapped.

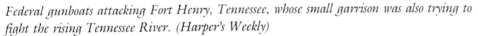

Federal gunboats attacking Fort Henry, Tennessee, whose small garrison was also trying to fight the rising Tennessee River. (Harper's Weekly)

On February 16, the Fort Donelson commander, Confederate general Simon Bolivar Buckner, raised a flag of truce and asked Grant what terms of surrender he would offer. "Unconditional surrender" was the firm reply. Buckner had no choice but to accept.

The fall of Fort Donelson was a major victory for the North. U. S. Grant had a new nickname, "Unconditional Surrender," to match his initials. The Federals gained control of middle Tennessee (including the state capital, Nashville). Fort Donelson yielded 13,000 Confederate prisoners—the largest number of U.S. prisoners of war captured until World War II.

A discouraged Johnston retreated through Tennessee to the rail junction at Corinth, Mississippi, just across the state line. While he gathered as many Confederate troops as he could, Grant's forces advanced southward up the Tennessee River. They halted and went into camp at Pittsburg Landing near the Tennessee-Mississippi border. Local folks called the place Shiloh, after a nearby meetinghouse.

Grant's intention was to wait there for another Federal army, under General Don Carlos Buell, to join him from Nashville. The combined Union forces would then attack Johnston's army, only twenty miles away at Corinth.

Johnston was aware of the Federal strategy. He determined to strike and destroy Grant before Buell could unite with him. The resulting battle of Shiloh, on April 6 and 7, was fought alongside the Tennessee River on a high wooded plateau cut with hollows and ravines.

The first Confederate attack caught Grant's men totally by surprise. Throughout a day of intense combat, the Federal line bent slowly back toward the river. Casualties were hundreds per hour. At the height of the fighting, General Sidney Johnston bled to death from a bullet wound.

Late that Sunday, the lead elements of Buell's force arrived on the field. Federals began their own attacks the next morning. The Confederates, with heavy losses and outnumbered two to one, abandoned the field. Weary and bloody, they made their way through driving rain back to Corinth.

Some 4,000 soldiers died at Shiloh. Four times that number fell wounded, and many died later from disease and poor medical treatment. More soldiers were killed or wounded at Shiloh than in any other battle in American history up to that time. The military results of the engagement were slight. However, each side knew that the other side could, and would, fight for as long as the war lasted.

THE MISSISSIPPI RIVER is the largest and longest stream in the United States. At the time of the Civil War, it was a mighty avenue cutting all the way through the Confederacy to the Gulf of Mexico. Union ships and soldiers would spend the first two years of the war securing the river piece by piece.

On April 8, the day after the battle of Shiloh ended, Federal forces under General John Pope gained an important victory on the Mississippi. A Confederate garrison manned Island No. 10, which protected an S-shaped curve in the river. Large numbers of Federals attacked the island fort. About 6,000 Confederates surrendered themselves and 150 cannon.

The fall of Island No. 10 enabled Northern troops to seize some eighty miles of the Mississippi River along the Tennessee border. Memphis fell to the Federals in early June. By the end of spring, all of Kentucky, half of Tennessee, and vital parts of Alabama and Mississippi were in Union hands.

On the western side of the Mississippi, other Federal units were tightening their hold. Three days of fighting in March at Pea Ridge, Arkansas, cleared Missouri of Confederate forces and secured northern Arkansas for the Union.

IN THE EAST that spring, Confederates managed to turn almost certain disaster into stunning victory.

Federal general McClellan had spent six months in Washington creating and training the mighty Army of the Potomac. Yet he seemed more interested in parades than in combat. President Lincoln finally had to order McClellan to advance his army against the Confederates. McClellan's "battle plan" called for no battle at all. He was going to win Richmond—and the war—by maneuver, much the way one wins a chess game.

Rather than march due south against the Confederate army, as McDowell had tried to do the previous summer, McClellan determined to take his large army to the coast of Virginia by boat. From there he would march westward across lightly defended country and capture the Southern capital.

In mid-March, some 70,000 Federals, 300 cannon, thousands of horses, and tons of supplies departed Washington by boat. More than 450 vessels of every shape and size eased their way down the Potomac River and Chesapeake Bay. They landed at Yorktown on the tip of the Virginia peninsula formed by the York and James rivers. The first shock McClellan received was that the Confederate army, thought to be up at Manassas, Virginia, was not there. It was on the peninsula, standing between McClellan and Richmond. Commanding that Southern army was General Joseph E. Johnston.

McClellan's forces began a cautious advance. On a rainy May 5, parts of the opposing forces fought an all-day battle at Williamsburg. The chief result of this clash was to slow down the already slow-moving McClellan. His army had swelled to 100,000 men. Johnston did not have half that number of soldiers. The Confederate general had to retreat toward Richmond. Rain fell every day in May as McClellan's huge army inched forward along every road and through every clearing on the peninsula.

On May 31, with Richmond only nine miles to his rear, Johnston attacked part of McClellan's force at Seven Pines (also called Fair Oaks). The Confederate assaults, strong but not in one great surge, stopped McClellan's advance. In the fighting, Johnston fell seriously wounded. President Jefferson Davis quickly appointed General Robert E. Lee to take charge of a Confederate army with its back almost at Richmond's door.

Lee was a desk general and adviser to President Davis at the time. Soon he would become one of the foremost field commanders in history. The best way to defend against an enemy, Lee thought, was to attack. He resolved to strike McClellan while the Union army stood still.

The Confederate general built up his forces as rapidly as he could. He sent his cavalry chief, the always colorful but sometimes reckless General James Ewell Brown ("Jeb") Stuart, to learn exactly where McClellan's northern flank ended. Stuart carried out his duty; then, for good measure, he and his 1,200 troopers rode completely past the rear of the Army of the Potomac, galloped by its southern flank, and rejoined Lee's army with many prisoners and much information.

Among the troops that Lee summoned to the defense of Richmond was General Stonewall Jackson's small army. Jackson had become a living legend that spring in the Shenandoah Valley. During the period from March 23 to June 9, Jackson swept back and forth in a campaign so daring and skillful that it is still studied today in most military schools around the world.

Jackson's infantry became known as foot cavalry because they seemed able to march as long and as far as mounted soldiers could ride. Outnumbered at times by four to one, Jackson's men tramped over 600 miles through the valley in forty-eight days, fought eleven engagements, defeated three separate Federal armies, and kept 60,000 additional Northern soldiers in Washington from joining McClellan. After that, Jackson led his men toward Richmond.

Lee's plan was to hit McClellan's flank from the west with his own army while Jackson delivered an attack from the northwest. The resulting Seven Days' Campaign began on June 26 and consisted of one sharp engagement after another. Driving from north to south across the peninsula, Lee pounded McClellan at Mechanicsville, Gaines' Mill, White Oak Swamp, Frayser's Farm, and Malvern Hill.

The first assaults by the military team of Lee and Jackson lacked good timing and concentration. The Confederates won only one of the battles. They suffered 20,000 casualties to McClellan's 16,500 losses. Yet Lee's soldiers literally pushed McClellan's army to the banks of the James River. Richmond, a proud capital on the brink of capture, was saved.

Late in July, a new Federal army under General John Pope left Washington. It passed through Manassas and began threatening Richmond from the north. Lee's forces remained badly outnumbered by McClellan's army. However, the Confederate commander sent Jackson's force from Richmond to hold off Pope while Lee watched for any new movements by McClellan.

On August 9, Jackson stopped Pope's drive in a hard battle at Cedar Mountain, near Culpeper. By then McClellan had received orders to abandon the peninsula and return to Washington with his Army of the Potomac. This retreat gave Lee the chance to join Jackson for a campaign against Pope.

Jackson then conducted one of the war's great marches. His men disappeared behind a range of mountains, reappeared in the rear of Pope's army, and destroyed the huge Federal supply depot at Manassas Junction. Pope angrily turned back and began a series of attacks against Jackson in a battle known as Second Manassas, or Second Bull Run.

Federals made repeated assaults against Jackson's entrenched divisions. Meanwhile, Lee put the other half of his army in motion. Leading those troops was General James Longstreet, a solemn officer whom Lee would soon call "my old war horse."

Longstreet managed to get his troops in position on the weak flank of the Union army without Pope being aware of it. The climax of Second Manassas came when Longstreet's troops attacked and all but overran Pope's lines. For a second time in little more than a year, the Union army had met with defeat along quiet Bull Run.

Virginia was free of a Federal army for the moment. The time was ripe, Lee stated boldly, to invade the North.

Carrying the war into Northern territory might force the Federals to ask for peace. Such an invasion could relieve the pressure on war-torn Virginia and give its farmers time to gather the meager autumn crops. A Southern success across the Potomac might be the lever to bring Maryland into the Confederacy—and it would leave Washington surrounded by enemy territory.

Most importantly, the Confederate government felt, one or two victories on Northern soil might persuade England or France to enter the contest on the side of the South. Foreign aid, as the colonists had discovered when France joined Americans in the Revolution, could mean final victory for the South.

The Confederate army was in high spirits when it waded across the Potomac River early in September, but happiness was short-lived. Maryland's citizens did not rally around the Southern army as expected.

Once again Lee found it necessary to divide his army, because Federals had reinforced Harpers Ferry, which they had seized earlier that year. Jackson and his divisions were directed to march back and capture Harpers Ferry. Control of it would ensure that the Shenandoah Valley avenue was open, should Lee have to retreat.

Meanwhile, McClellan and his Federal army were in slow pursuit. A Union soldier happened to find a copy of Lee's marching orders. But even with that valuable information, the ever-cautious McClellan did not move promptly. The Union commander's delays gave Lee time to pull his army together for battle.

On Wednesday, September 17, the two principal armies in the war met in combat. The battlefield was along the banks of Antietam Creek near the village of Sharpsburg, Maryland. Fighting began at dawn and did not stop for fourteen hours. McClellan failed to use his superior numbers in a massive assault all along the Confederate line. He sent his troops into action in separate attacks at daybreak, noon, and midafternoon.

Lee managed to hold his ground most of the day by shifting men from one sector to another. Places on the field such as the Dunkard Church, East Woods, Bloody Lane, and Burnside's Bridge were scenes of shocking losses on both sides.

ABOVE: *Burnside's Bridge, Antietam, 1862. This postwar painting, known as a lithograph, shows a much cleaner and more orderly battle than was the case. Burnside's Bridge still stands on the battlefield. (Abby Aldrich Rockefeller Folk Art Collection).*

LEFT: *Union general Ambrose Burnside. The word* sideburns *comes from his massive whiskers. (National Archives)*

Late in the afternoon, Lee's line seemed about to break. At that moment, General Ambrose Powell Hill's Confederate division rushed onto the field after a rapid seventeen-mile march from Harpers Ferry. Hill's unexpected attack on the Federal troops of General Ambrose Everett Burnside shattered the Federal left flank. Darkness mercifully ended the bloodiest day in American history.

Some 4,800 dead soldiers lay sprawled on the ground across the four-mile-long battlefield. Another 18,500 men were wounded, and 3,000 of them would die in the crude field hospitals nearby. Lee's army then limped back to Virginia. Although he had fought McClellan to a draw at Antietam Creek, the battle had long-range consequences.

Lincoln used the failure of Lee's invasion to announce a plan he had been considering for several weeks. Slavery in the United States had to end, the Northern president felt. To accomplish that goal in the easiest way possible, Lincoln issued the Emancipation Proclamation as a military measure for ending the war.

The proclamation promised freedom to all slaves in the Confederate states that did not return to the Union by January 1, 1863. From that time forward, the North would have two war aims: to restore the Union and to lift the chains of bondage from millions of black people in the Confederacy.

While Lee was moving through Maryland, the Confederate army in the western theater also launched an invasion. The death of General Sidney Johnston at Shiloh led to the appointment of General Braxton Bragg as new commander of the South's Army of Tennessee.

Bragg was a stern officer: gruff, unfriendly, and given to arguing constantly with his officers. Strict obedience to orders was his answer to every problem. In combat he displayed a habit of starting with good intentions but stumbling from one battle to another. He first demonstrated those traits in the summer and autumn of 1862.

By August the Confederate forces of generals Bragg and Edmund Kirby Smith had reoccupied most of middle Tennessee. The two generals led their troops into Kentucky by separate routes. Smith's forces gained an easy victory at Richmond in the eastern part of the state. Bragg succeeded as well, capturing 4,000 Federals at Munfordville, Kentucky. The Confederates were now in a position to march to the Ohio River and occupy Louisville, Kentucky's most important city. Only one obstacle threatened their advance—Buell's Federal army, rushing north back into Kentucky.

Bragg wasted days trying to set up a Confederate government in Kentucky. He should have given attention to the Federal army. Bragg also should have united the two wings of his own forces once he was in hostile territory. On October 8, Union and Confederate armies collided at Perryville, Kentucky. It was a battle fought for water. The whole countryside was suffering from a drought, but there were a few pools of water in the Perryville area.

This largest of Civil War battles in Kentucky was a series of mistakes by both Bragg and Buell. The Confederates attacked first and drove back the Federals. Union troops then made assaults and forced the Southerners from the field. More than 7,600 total casualties occurred at Perryville. For all of that bloodshed, the engagement had no meaning in the long run.

Bragg's outnumbered army, divided and weak, was exposed to assault from all directions in Kentucky. Bragg and Smith combined their forces and secured large amounts of supplies in Kentucky before returning to Tennessee. As with Lee in Maryland, Bragg's offensive had begun with high hopes and ended with disappointing results.

Elsewhere that autumn, especially along the Mississippi River, Confederates suffered other reverses. On August 5, a Southern attack at Baton Rouge, Louisiana, failed. The next month, Confederate armies met defeat at Iuka, Mississippi, and Newtonia, Missouri. Early October brought still another setback, this time after two days of fighting at Corinth, Mississippi. On December 7, a Federal force at Prairie Grove, Arkansas, soundly thrashed its Confederate opponents. The North was slowly tightening a noose around the Confederacy. Still, the Southern nation demonstrated in the final month of 1862 that it was alive and quite capable of inflicting severe damage.

Cold weather was settling over the country when Grant's army began moving out of Tennessee toward Vicksburg, Mississippi, the last major Confederate defense on the Mississippi River. Located on high bluffs overlooking a sharp bend in the river, Vicksburg had become a hill fortress. It was strongly manned by Confederate troops.

Grant's plan was for his colleague and close friend William T. Sherman to take his part of the army downriver by boat and attack the northern defenses of Vicksburg. Grant would move overland with the rest of his army and attack at the same time as Sherman. It was a good plan, but Grant forgot about the threat of Confederate cavalry to the rear.

Federal troops were marching in relaxed fashion toward Vicksburg when Southern horsemen burst into Grant's supply base at Holly Springs, Mississippi, and destroyed most of Grant's stores. A force of 1,200 Confederate troopers under General Nathan Bedford Forrest tore up railroads and burned Federal supplies. They captured 4,000 soldiers as well as 10,000 muskets as they galloped across Union-held Tennessee.

These setbacks forced Grant to abandon his march to Vicksburg. Sherman was left without added support to make a hopeless attack against strongly entrenched Southerners. He lost 1,800 men to the Confederates' 200 in the December 28–29 fighting at Chickasaw Bayou.

Two weeks earlier, in Virginia, Robert E. Lee had won one of the most lopsided victories of the war. McClellan's repeated failures to push after Lee following Antietam Creek had forced Lincoln to replace him in November at the head of the Army of the Potomac. The new commander was General Ambrose Burnside, a former corps commander who had not performed well seven weeks earlier at Antietam.

On December 13, Burnside ordered assaults against Lee's heavily fortified lines on the hills behind Fredericksburg, Virginia. Fourteen times Union troops charged across the open ground. "We might as well have tried to take Hell," a Federal soldier later wrote. By nightfall the Union army had suffered 12,600 losses. Many of the wounded froze to death where they fell. "It is well that war is so terrible," Lee commented at one point in the battle. Otherwise, "we should grow too fond of it."

The final fighting of 1862 began on the last day of the year at Murfreesboro, Tennessee. General William Starke Rosecrans, who replaced Buell in command of the western Federal army, had moved south from Nashville to confront Bragg's Confederate forces. For three days, along Stones River near Murfreesboro, the two armies fought it out mostly in open country.

Confederates were victorious in the first day's fighting, but after that Bragg's attacks met concentrated fire from Union cannon and muskets. The battle of Murfreesboro ended with both sides battered. Bragg and Rosecrans each lost a third of their armies. The Confederate withdrawal from the field signaled a Northern victory. Rosecrans remained in control of the Nashville area.

On the night before this great battle began, soldiers blue and gray sat huddled in the cold darkness. Only a few yards separated the opposing lines. The men began singing songs together to pass the time. No tune was sung louder, or felt more deeply, than "Home, Sweet Home."

The year 1862 ended. Bloodshed rather than brotherhood had become the American way of life.

The struggle at Stones River, Tennessee—sometimes called the battle of Murfreesboro—raged for three days in freezing weather. (Battles and Leaders of the Civil War)

Waving Banners

A flag is the most visible symbol of a nation. In the Civil War, armies on both sides marched and fought with the colors in front. One of the most popular fighting songs of that day contained the words "Yes, we'll rally 'round the flag, boys, we'll rally once again . . ."

In the beginning of the war, Federal forces used the traditional Stars and Stripes as their national flag. The flag had thirty-four stars—one for each state of the Union—and the North continued to include the Confederate states on the flag even though they had seceded. Inside the canton—the square in the upper corner—the stars were arranged in two rows of seven stars each at the top, two rows of seven stars each at the bottom, and a row of six stars in the middle.

The 1863 admission of West Virginia to the Union meant that a new star had to be added. It was placed in the center row. Thereafter, the Stars and Stripes bore five rows of seven stars each.

Confederates never considered any other color combination for their flag but red, white, and blue. Several Southern banners were proposed in the course of the war. Two particular Confederate flags enjoyed widespread use. The national flag was called the Stars and Bars. It had three horizontal bars of red, white, and red. Its blue canton had a circle of seven white stars representing the original states of the Confederacy. Later versions of the Stars and Bars had eleven and then thirteen stars. The official size of the flag was 64 inches long and 36 inches wide, but banners of smaller size were used most often.

At the 1861 battle of First Manassas, Southern soldiers found that the Stars and Bars looked too much like the Stars and Stripes, especially when the wind was not blowing. A new flag appeared shortly thereafter. It was called the Southern Cross, and it became the Confederate battle flag.

Unlike modern-day and so-called Confederate flags, the Southern Cross was square. It had a red field, with a cross of blue extending to each of the four corners. Inside the cross were thirteen stars. They represented the eleven Confederate States, with two stars added for Kentucky and Missouri in the hope that those two states would someday be part of the Southern nation.

The Stars and Bars, official flag of the Confederacy. (Harper's Weekly)

Southern Cross. (West Point Museum)

8

Grant, Lee, and Other Commanders

CIVIL WAR BATTLES produced more unforgettable generals than any other struggle in the nation's history. One reason for this, of course, is that both sides were American. Every commander became part of our heritage.

The conflict of the 1860s also involved a larger proportion of the population than any other American war. More soldiers had the chance to develop their talents. The nineteenth century was an age without computers, electronics, and all that we call current technology. Generals were much closer to their men. They led by example and personality. Because these officers were more involved with their troops, they are better remembered.

When the Civil War began, a third of the officers in the U.S. Army resigned their posts and joined the Confederacy. Some 350 men who had attended West Point, as well as 225 graduates of the Virginia Military Institute and 200 officers who were products of other military schools in the South, all offered their swords to the Confederate States. This gave the Southern nation about 700 professional soldiers of officer rank to lead the Rebel armies. About the same number of available officers existed in the North.

The large armies of that day required many generals. In all, there were 583 Federal and 425 Confederate generals. However, barely 300 of them had served in the prewar army. The large majority came from two basic classes.

First were the "political generals"—prominent politicians or civic leaders who received an appointment as general because of their political influence rather than their military ability. With few exceptions, these men proved to be costly misfits at the head of troops. It is impossible to know how many hundreds of soldiers died as a result of their poor leadership. Yet both governments continued to make generals out of politicians for at least the first half of the war.

"Civilian generals" formed the second large group of nonprofessional officers. They were men who entered the army at a lower rank and, largely by heroism in battle, won promotion to general. Georgia's most distinguished soldier belonged to that group. John Brown Gordon began his service as captain of a Georgia company. By 1865, he was a senior major general in Lee's army. Confederate general Nathan Bedford Forrest, one of the most brilliant cavalry commanders of all time, enlisted in 1861 as a private.

Men could become generals by appointment or by advancement. The North in particular followed a custom of brevet promotions, which today are known as battlefield commissions. By this method, an officer could be promoted immediately to a temporary rank that might or might not become permanent at a later date.

Some incredible brevet promotions were given in the Civil War. The most dramatic occurred in June 1863 when First Lieutenant George Armstrong Custer leaped five ranks in a single jump to the grade of brigadier general.

When one looks at photographs of the bearded generals of the 1860s, it is natural to think that they were elderly men with many years of experience. That is not the case at all. Most officers in that war wore beards,

Federal lieutenant George A. Custer (RIGHT) *and his West Point classmate Confederate lieutenant John A. Washington, who had been captured in action. (Library of Congress)*

not only because it was the style but also to conceal their shocking youthfulness. A typical brigadier general was only thirty-seven years old. As the conflict continued, the generals seemed to get younger.

Galusha Pennypacker of Pennsylvania was the youngest of all Civil War general officers. He became a Federal captain at the age of sixteen. Valor and five battle wounds brought him promotion to brigadier general in February 1865. Pennypacker was still too young to vote, but he was a general at the age of twenty.

John Herbert Kelly of Alabama was the youngest Confederate general. Born in 1840, he attended West Point before entering the Southern army. Kelly rose steadily through the ranks until his November 1863 appointment as a brigadier. He was twenty-three. Ten months later, Kelly was killed in action.

This was truly a "brother's war" for many generals. It was a family tragedy for other commanders. Federal general Philip St. George Cooke fought against his son, Confederate general John Rogers Cooke, and against his son-in-law, General Jeb Stuart. Union general George Gordon Meade was a brother-in-law of Confederate general Henry Alexander Wise. Two sons of Senator John Jordan Crittenden of Kentucky became generals on opposite sides. James Barbour Terrill fell dead in battle on the day before the Confederate Congress approved his promotion to general. His brother, Federal general William Rufus Terrill, was killed in action eighteen months earlier. Almost every general in the Civil War had a relative or close friend on the other side.

When the war began, the South had better generals than the North. In fact, the history of the Confederacy is the story of its military leaders. The "flower of Southern manhood" went into the armies and brought glory to the Confederacy. A combination of battle losses on the Southern side and the emergence of capable, hard-hitting commanders on the Federal side swung the advantage to the North midway through the struggle. Union generals became stronger and better in the war's last years.

Something else makes this shift of leadership interesting. Not a single Federal commander of importance in 1861 was still in a command position in 1865. The Union generals who stood so tall when the war ended were fairly unknown in the first stages of the conflict.

Ulysses S. Grant (1822–1885) was such a latecomer. He was graduated from West Point in 1843, fought well in the Mexican War, but was

LEFT: *At five feet seven inches tall, and weighing 135 pounds, Ulysses S. Grant hardly looked the part of the victorious Federal general. (Library of Congress)*
BELOW: *Inside one of the earthworks at Atlanta, Georgia, Federal general Sherman sits astride his favorite horse, Sam. (National Archives)*

forced from the army in 1854 because of charges that he drank too much. Grant tried a number of civilian jobs before going to work in his father's leather-goods store. In 1861, he took command of a Federal regiment from Illinois and headed south into history.

Grant hardly looked the part of a great general. Shy, short in stature, round-shouldered, with a reddish beard cropped closely on his weathered face, Sam Grant said little and kept a cigar in his mouth most of the time. However, a staff officer noted, Grant's usual expression was that of a man who had made up his mind to drive his head through a stone wall.

Determination was one of his greatest qualities. A Confederate general who knew him well said of Grant in 1864: "That man will fight us every day and every hour until the end of the war." He did just that, beginning with Fort Henry and Fort Donelson. Grant moved from victory to victory and is regarded as the general who won the Civil War. In 1868, he was elected to the first of two terms as president of the United States.

Grant was not a military genius who took brilliant gambles and made flashing strikes. His position as one of America's premier field commanders was the result of more solid qualities: a wide vision of the war and what had to be done to win, balanced judgment, dogged courage, common sense, and good luck at the right times. Midway in the war, President Lincoln paid Grant one of the highest compliments: "I can't spare this man; he fights."

Tall and lean, General William T. Sherman (1820–1891) was Grant's most trusted officer and an outstanding field commander. Soldiers called Sherman "Uncle Billy" and "Cump." Like Grant, Sherman was a West Point graduate who left the army in the 1850s. He was superintendent of a Louisiana military academy before becoming a successful St. Louis businessman. Sherman returned to the army at the outbreak of civil war and steadily advanced to become one of the North's leading generals.

Sherman the soldier was not a likable man. Unkempt hair and beard surrounded a face that was naturally grim and frowning, and there was always a wild expression in his eyes. He disliked newspapermen, whom he accused of being unable to tell the truth. Sherman was also convinced from the beginning that the Civil War was going to be long and hard. In 1861, when Lincoln issued the first call for 75,000 men to serve for three months, Sherman snorted: "You might as well attempt to put out the flames of a burning house with a squirt gun."

He fought in cold-blooded fashion, with a "terrible swift sword" that would make his name a bitter word in the South for generations to come.

Another no-nonsense general in the North was Philip Henry Sheridan (1831–1888). He was graduated from West Point near the bottom of his class, then served at various frontier posts until civil war gave him a chance to display his full military abilities. "Little Phil" Sheridan was a tough man, only five feet five inches tall, with hard eyes and a bullet-shaped head. His uniform was always mud-spattered. He wore a flat black hat that seemed at least two sizes too small for him. Sheridan rode a horse at breakneck speed. Given to cursing and shouting, he had no patience with timid officers who made excuses. His well-deserved reputation as a hard fighter made him one of the most dependable of Civil War generals.

George B. McClellan (1826–1885) was Sheridan's opposite in almost every way. From the time he was graduated at the top of his West Point class, he displayed a brilliant mind. His prewar career as an engineer, West

Federal general George B. McClellan. Many officers of the day posed for photographs by placing a hand inside their jacket as French emperor Napoleon Bonaparte had done. (Library of Congress)

Philip H. Sheridan (BELOW), *the general on whom Grant most depended in the last year of the war. (National Archives)*

Point professor, western explorer, and inventor of a saddle that bears his name all stamped him as one of the most promising of army officers. He was only thirty-five when, in July 1861, Lincoln chose him to take command of all Federal forces in the East.

Handsome and confident, "Little Mac" proved to be the most skillful army organizer of the Civil War. He personally created the Army of the Potomac, equipped it, trained it, and gave it deep pride and high morale. But McClellan's good points were not enough to balance his weaknesses. Boastful and overly ambitious, he would pose for photographs with one hand inside his coat as Napoleon Bonaparte had done. And he proved to be a field commander who lacked any enthusiasm for battle.

Doubting himself, worried about the strength of his opponents, fearful of defeat, he was never eager to send his massive army into battle. Forced by Lincoln to advance on Richmond in 1862, McClellan found one excuse after another to avoid fighting. He then had to retreat in the face of Confederate attacks. At Antietam Creek later that year, McClellan failed to take advantage of his superior numbers and at best won only a draw.

Lincoln removed McClellan from command a few weeks later. The general saw no further military service. McClellan remains today one of the most controversial commanders of the Civil War.

THE CONFEDERACY died in 1865, but several of its generals have everlasting fame.

High on any list of great commanders is Virginia-born Robert E. Lee (1807–1870). He stands among the greatest soldiers in American history. Lee's father was Henry "Light-Horse Harry" Lee of Revolutionary War fame. After being graduated second in the West Point class of 1829, Robert Lee became one of the army's best engineers. He won three brevet promotions for gallantry in the Mexican War.

A tour of duty as superintendent of West Point followed. Lee then returned to field service and became second-in-command of the 2nd U.S. Cavalry, the army's crack unit. In 1859, he commanded the troops who captured John Brown's band at Harpers Ferry.

Lee deeply loved the Union and had no strong feelings for slavery. Lincoln offered him supreme command of all Federal armies. But Lee resigned from the army rather than raise his sword against his native state. When Virginia joined the Confederacy, Lee did the same.

Robert E. Lee sat for this photograph a few days after surrendering his army in 1865. (Library of Congress)

Placed in command of Virginia's forces in the first months of the war, Lee organized them well. Assignments as a Confederate general and military adviser to President Davis followed. Lee attended to paperwork and special duties until June 1, 1862, when he was appointed to command the Army of Northern Virginia. The Civil War was a year old before Lee saw his first service in the field.

For three years thereafter, Lee demonstrated the resourcefulness, character, and genius of a brilliant army leader. He could attack savagely and was a master of defense. Lee defended Virginia as no other general could have done. Even in the final months of the war, when Lee's army was half-starved, ragged, and ill-equipped, he inflicted three times the number of casualties on the Federals as he suffered.

Always bold, and always quick to strike, Lee was sometimes a bit reckless in his attacks. At times he placed too much trust in some generals who did not deserve that confidence.

Lee the man was modest, religious, kind, and courteous. He rarely raised his voice in anger. His favorite expressions for the enemy were "those people" and "our friends across the river." This Virginia general was a handsome man of above-average height. The Civil War turned his hair gray and then ruined his health.

When surrender came, Confederate soldiers poured out their love and grief for Lee as much as for the South. A Southern officer described the scene when Lee rode back into his lines after agreeing to terms with Grant:

> When [our troops] saw the well-known figure of General Lee approaching, there was a general rush from each side of the road to greet him as he passed . . . As soon as Lee entered this avenue of these soldiers—the men who had stood their duty through thick and thin in so many battles—wild heartfelt cheers arose which so touched General Lee that tears filled his eyes and trickled down his cheeks . . . This exhibition of feeling on his part found quick response from the men, whose cheers changed to choking sobs. . . . Grim, bearded men threw themselves on the ground, covered their faces with their hands, and wept like children.

Thomas J. "Stonewall" Jackson (1824–1863) ranks second only to Lee as a Southern legend. Born in the mountains of western Virginia, orphaned at an early age, Jackson entered West Point and had to study constantly to keep up with his better-prepared classmates. In 1851, he left the army to become a professor at Virginia Military Institute. The large, well-built Jackson was a poor teacher but a stickler for discipline. He was cold, reserved, and lacking in humor. Cadets called him "Tom Fool" Jackson or simply "the Major."

It was during the VMI years that Jackson joined the Presbyterian church.

Religion quickly became the core of his life. He attended every church service; he would not read a newspaper or write a letter on Sunday. In the Civil War, when forced to fight a battle on Sunday, Jackson evaded this violation of devotion by issuing an order assigning another day of the week for worship services. Everything he did was for the glory of God.

Jackson entered Confederate service in April 1861 and soon took command of a brigade of Shenandoah Valley soldiers. He, and they, acquired the name "Stonewall" for their strong stand at the battle of First Manassas. The following spring, Jackson greatly enhanced his reputation with his campaign in the Shenandoah Valley. His victory at Second Manassas a few months later added to his fame. "Old Jack" and his "foot cavalry" thrilled the Southern people by their actions. Even Federal generals looked on Jackson with a mixture of amazement and fear.

Secrecy of plans, great sweeping flank marches, and pounding attacks were the keys to Jackson's brilliance. He brought success to the South at a time when the South badly needed success. Many officers thought him too quiet, stern, and demanding. Jackson did not care what men thought. He was fighting for God, and that was all that mattered.

In 1863, after he had been in the field only two years, Jackson was accidentally shot by his own men at Chancellorsville. He died of pneumo-

LEFT: *Confederate general Stonewall Jackson, who fought as if on a religious crusade.* (Library of Congress)
OPPOSITE, LEFT: *Jeb Stuart, commander of Confederate cavalry in Lee's army. (Library of Congress)*
OPPOSITE, RIGHT: *Nathan Bedford Forrest, one of the Confederacy's best-thinking and hardest-driving cavalrymen. (Museum of the Confederacy)*

nia a week later. His death was the heaviest blow the Confederacy suffered during the entire war.

James E. B. Stuart (1833–1864) was the very picture of a romantic cavalier. This West Point graduate became the most famous cavalry leader in Virginia. He was at his best in gathering information on enemy movements. Stuart wore a huge beard, a flashy uniform, and a feather in his hat. He fought in the daredevil manner of a confident cavalry leader.

On May 11, 1864, Stuart was mortally wounded in a cavalry fight outside Richmond. He died the following day. Lee's cavalry was never as effective thereafter.

The greatest cavalry leader on either side in the Civil War was Nathan Bedford Forrest (1821–1877). A self-made man with but six months' total schooling, Forrest became a wealthy Tennessee planter and slave dealer. He joined the Confederate army as a private but rose to a general's rank within a year.

Beginning in 1862, Forrest and his troopers ranged through Tennessee, Alabama, and Mississippi. "Old Bedford" had never seen a military book, and he would not have understood one if he had tried to read it. Forrest performed one lightning stroke after another with a combination of instinct and imagination. His technique was always the same: gallop deep

into enemy territory, surprise the foe, strike furiously, cause heavy destruction, and then ride away before the victims could recover their balance.

Forrest was dark-haired, always serious, and blunt in language. He cared nothing for personal safety. During the war twenty-nine horses were shot from under him. Forrest himself was wounded three times. He personally killed or wounded at least thirty Federals in hand-to-hand combat.

Forrest's exploits were so many and so spectacular that myths sprang up around him. One report in 1864 had him in Canada and about to raid Chicago, Illinois, 500 miles from where he actually was.

Once, when asked why he was such a good cavalryman, the poorly educated Forrest is supposed to have replied: "I gits thar fustest with the mostest." That is not a true story, but his great cavalry raids prevented the Federals from gaining complete control of the western theater for most of the war.

Joseph E. Johnston (1807–1891) was a West Point classmate of Robert E. Lee. In the Mexican War, Johnston received five wounds and came home a hero. By 1861, he was quartermaster general, in charge of supplies for the U.S. Army.

"Uncle Joe" led the Army of Northern Virginia until he fell seriously wounded at the 1862 battle of Seven Pines. A year later, he was assigned to lead the Army of Tennessee. In both the eastern and western theaters, Johnston was dangerous in combat. A Federal officer once remarked: "Beware of Lee's advances and Johnston's retreats." Confederate troops trusted him; Federal commanders respected him. Johnston was a stubborn and overly proud commander, and he and President Davis argued bitterly during the war—and to the end of their lives.

Leading men into combat is a basic part of warfare. The length and the outcome of any struggle depend in great part on the quality of leadership in the opposing armies. The Civil War was two years old before the Union found the generals who would fight the kind of pounding, total war the South could not resist. The small and weak Confederacy lasted four years because of the brilliance in battle of its field commanders.

The Lees and Jacksons of the South were skillful at old-fashioned war, in which quick maneuvers and sudden strikes meant success. The Grants and Shermans were the first of the modern generals, who believed in using heavy numbers of men and constant pressure to defeat the enemy. In the 1860s the North could wage that new kind of war. The South could not.

9

War on the Waters

THE CIVIL WAR began and ended at sea. In January 1861, South Carolina batteries fired on the *Star of the West* as that vessel sought to bring provisions to the Federal garrison at Fort Sumter. Nearly five years later the crew of the CSS *Shenandoah* became the last group of Confederates to surrender.

Creating a navy was a major task for both sides in the Civil War. In 1861, the U.S. Navy consisted of only forty-two ships. They were scattered all over the globe. The Confederate navy was in even worse shape. A few vessels were seized when the Southern coastal states left the Union, and 230 of the navy's 1,420 officers resigned to serve in the Confederacy. That was not much of a start for fighting a war.

Lincoln knew nothing about naval affairs, but he was well aware of how valuable a strong navy could be in the struggle. Less than a week after the firing on Fort Sumter, Lincoln announced that in order to protect the "public peace," he was ordering a blockade of all ports in the South. The man chosen to organize the blockade was Secretary of the Navy Gideon Welles. Possessing real talent for navy building, Welles began working at once and never slowed down.

The main shipbuilding yards were in the North. Most of the cargo-carrying vessels were Northern-owned. Welles bought or rented every seaworthy craft he could obtain to help close off the Southern ports. So strong a naval leader did Welles become that he was known affectionately as the "Old Man of the Sea."

The U.S. Navy jumped from 42 ships in 1861 to 671 by 1864. As important as the increase in numbers was the increase in quality. The navy went from old wooden sailing vessels to new craft ranging from ironclad warships to specially built river gunboats to huge transports for carrying troops. Thus, while the Union blockade was not effective at first, it grew stronger with each passing month.

In the beginning, the blockading ships along the Atlantic coast had to return to Federal-held Hampton Roads, Virginia, or Key West, Florida, for repairs and supplies, a 600-mile voyage for many of the vessels. Therefore, many blockade ships spent more time going to and from their bases than they did on blockade duty.

The navy determined to solve this problem by gaining one toehold after another along the Confederate coast. In the summer of 1861, joint army-navy expeditions began to attack small Southern inlets and harbors. This hopscotching movement continued along the coastline until, by the spring of 1862, Federal bases existed at such vital points as Roanoke Island, North Carolina; Port Royal, South Carolina; Fort Pulaski, Georgia; and Ship Island, Mississippi.

In the first half of the Civil War, small coasting vessels, with limited cargo obtained in Havana, Bermuda, and Nassau, regularly sailed into

To build up its naval forces blockading the Southern coast, Federal recruiters used posters such as this for the enlistment of sailors. (The Bettmann Archive)

Southern ports not under blockade. As Northern blockaders increased in number, running the blockade became more difficult. By 1864, the South was relying heavily on foreign-built blockade-runners: light, low-lying ships capable of short bursts of speed as they dashed through the ring of U.S. Navy blockaders. Federal warships captured or sank 150 blockade-runners during the war. They never succeeded in stopping the trade completely, but they did enough damage to cripple a South already limping from lack of supplies.

At the same time, Federal ships played an important role in the western theater, especially in gaining control of the all-important Mississippi River. In April 1862, naval commander David G. Farragut steamed into the mouth of the big river. His goal was New Orleans. Farragut's small fleet, its guns blazing, fought its way past two Confederate forts. Federal sailors suffered heavy losses (39 killed and 171 wounded), but they got past the forts and captured now-helpless New Orleans.

Much of the story of the river war in the West revolves around joint army-navy operations. Federal successes in 1862 at Fort Henry, Fort Donelson, and Island No. 10 demonstrated the advantages of combining ships and infantry. The most remarkable activity of the Union fleets on the western waters would come in 1863 with action against the Confederate stronghold at Vicksburg, Mississippi.

Stephen R. Mallory was the Confederate secretary of the navy. A former senator from Florida, Mallory was capable and farsighted. He realized from the start that the South could not hope to match the North ship for ship. It never did. The South put about 130 vessels into use. Most of them were small craft mounting no more than one or two guns, because nowhere in the Confederacy was there a foundry that could manufacture a steam engine large enough to propel a full-size warship.

Mallory concluded that he had to develop new ideas and new instruments if the Southern nation was to hold off the U.S. Navy's great wooden fleets. The decision was made to experiment with something brand-new: ironclad ships.

The first such vessel took shape in the winter of 1861–1862 at Norfolk, Virginia. Southern shipbuilders converted the wooden frigate USS *Merrimack* into an awesome-looking iron battleship. Confederates named their creation the CSS *Virginia*. It was 262 feet long and covered with sloping iron plates. This new Southern battleship packed ten heavy guns and carried a crew of 350 men. The *Virginia*'s captain was Franklin Buchanan, who had been the first superintendent of the U.S. Naval Academy at Annapolis, Maryland.

On March 8, 1862, the *Virginia* steamed into the great Norfolk harbor known as Hampton Roads. It destroyed the Union ships *Congress* and *Cumberland* and ran three others aground. Happy Confederate sailors looked forward to sinking the Federal flagship *Minnesota* the following day.

The U.S. Navy had also been constructing an ironclad vessel. It arrived at Norfolk on the night the Confederates were celebrating.

The Union ship looked like nothing anyone had ever seen before. At 175 feet in length, the USS *Monitor* was smaller than the *Virginia*. Only two feet of the *Monitor*'s hull was above water. Iron five inches thick covered the boat. The vessel resembled a long floating raft with a revolving turret on top. Two powerful eleven-inch rifled guns were inside the turret. This black monster was officially called the USS *Monitor*. Sailors referred to it as a "tin can on a shingle."

For two hours on Sunday, March 9, the *Monitor* and the *Virginia* exchanged fire at close quarters. Dozens of cannon balls bounced off the iron-plated hulls with loud, echoing clangs. One of the junior officers aboard the *Virginia* ordered some of his guns to cease firing. When asked by his commander why he had stopped firing at the *Monitor,* the officer replied: "Our powder is precious. . . . I find that I can do her about as much damage by snapping my thumb at her every two minutes and a half!"

The *Virginia* then tried to ram the *Monitor*. But the small engines on the *Virginia* produced only enough speed for the big ironclad to bump the *Monitor* several times. For six hours these two vessels delivered every blow they had. Neither one could do serious damage to the other. The duel of ironclads was a draw. However, that March 9 fight clearly signaled that the age of wooden battleships had ended.

Both the *Virginia* and the *Monitor* had short lives. Two months after the famous duel, a large Federal fleet trapped the *Virginia* inside the Norfolk harbor. Confederate sailors destroyed the vessel rather than let it be captured. On the last day of 1862, the *Monitor* sank in a gale off Cape Hatteras, North Carolina.

Throughout the war the Confederates tried to put a number of ironclads into action. However, the South's resources were too limited to permit the construction of more than half a dozen such ships. On the

Neither the USS Monitor (LEFT) *or the CSS* Virginia (RIGHT) *could destroy the other, but their 1862 battle marked the birth of ironclad warships around the world. (Battles and Leaders of the Civil War)*

Mississippi River, the homemade ironclad ram *Arkansas* all but fell apart in its second engagement. The *Albemarle,* operating on the Roanoke River in North Carolina, enjoyed a measure of success until Federal sailors destroyed it in a commando-like operation.

In the summer of 1864, a powerful Federal fleet under Admiral Farragut steamed into the harbor at Mobile, Alabama, with guns firing furiously. Confederates had mined the channel, but Farragut sent in his ships with the now-famous battle cry "Damn the torpedoes! Full speed ahead!"

The eighteen Union ships (including four ironclads of the *Monitor* class) had barely entered Mobile Bay when they came face-to-face with a single but huge Confederate ironclad, the *Tennessee.* For three hours the *Tennessee* fought alone. Its fire raked the Federal ships and did much damage. However, heavy gunfire from Farragut's vessels battered the Confederate ironclad. With its smokestack shot away, its engine barely running, two of its guns put out of action, and the captain wounded, the *Tennessee* finally lowered its colors in surrender.

Confederate naval officials were painfully aware that they lacked the money and facilities to build a large fleet. They tried a number of revolutionary experiments in naval warfare. Especially successful were underwater mines, then called torpedoes. Matthew Fontaine Maury, now known as the "Father of Oceanography," took charge of mining the James River in Virginia. As a result of Maury's skilled work, the Federal navy never threatened Richmond. The mines floated just beneath the surface and exploded on contact. They sank or damaged forty-three Union ships during the war.

Another new weapon developed by the Confederacy was the torpedo boat. This small, half-submerged, cigar-shaped vessel carried a long beam that extended from the bow, or front, of the ship. At the end of this beam was a torpedo—a thin metal can filled with gunpowder. The torpedo exploded when it struck its target. Had the South been able to produce torpedo boats on a greater scale, they might have been more than just a dangerous nuisance to Federal warships.

The most dramatic of all Confederate naval experiments was the con-

Torpedoes, as underwater mines were then called, floated just beneath the water's surface and exploded on contact with a ship. One torpedo could easily sink a wooden vessel of the day. (Harper's Weekly)

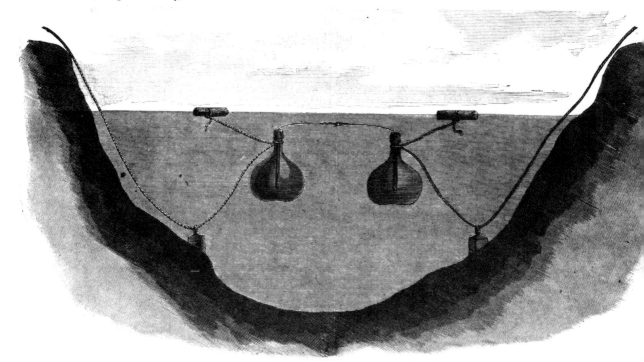

A painting of the H. L. Hunley, *history's first attack submarine. (Museum of the Confederacy)*

struction of history's first attack submarine. The *H.L. Hunley* (named after its inventor) was only thirty feet long and four feet wide. It carried a crew of nine men. Eight of them turned handles that operated the propeller; the skipper piloted the craft by means of a small wheel. A copper torpedo with ninety pounds of gunpowder was the *Hunley's* only weapon. To destroy an enemy vessel, the submarine had to ram its torpedo into the side of the ship. Crewmen would light the fuse to the torpedo, after which the submarine was supposed to back away to safety.

Disaster marked every trial run of the *Hunley*. Four times it made a practice cruise; four times it sank. A total of thirty-two men, including Hunley himself, suffocated or drowned in these first tests. Nevertheless, work continued on the strange vessel.

Its moment of glory came on February 17, 1864, in the harbor of Charleston, South Carolina. Manned by a new crew, the *Hunley* eased from her berth under cover of darkness and made for the Union blockading fleet. The target was the USS *Housatonic*, a powerful ship mounting twenty-three guns.

Around 9:00 P.M., the *Hunley* rammed her charge into the side of the *Housatonic*. A tremendous explosion ripped open the hull of the Federal ship. It sank quickly. So did the *Hunley,* apparently a victim of her own torpedo charge. The submarine has never been found.

The Confederate navy's prestige on the high seas came from several fast, heavily armed cruisers that roamed the oceans alone in search of Federal vessels. No more than eighteen such ships existed, but they achieved victories far beyond their small numbers by destroying 257 enemy cargo vessels.

The most famous of these Confederate raiders was the English-built *Alabama*. Its two 300-horsepower engines enabled it to run at thirteen knots (about eleven miles per hour), which was extremely fast for that day. Commanding the *Alabama* was the swashbuckling Raphael Semmes. His waxed mustachio and jaunty air seemed appropriate for his position. The *Alabama*'s 144-man crew was a mixture of English adventurers and Southern sailors. Semmes called them a "precious set of rascals."

During its two-year cruise, the *Alabama* seized about seventy ships. It prowled the Atlantic Ocean and even captured vessels in the China Sea and the Indian Ocean. The end of the *Alabama* came in June 1864 after the raider had stopped at Cherbourg, France, to take on supplies and fuel. Suddenly on the horizon appeared the USS *Kearsarge.*

The battle between the two ships began seven miles offshore and lasted an hour. Back and forth the two vessels steamed, firing broadside after broadside at a distance of barely a half mile. But the *Kearsarge* had heavier armor and forced the *Alabama* to strike its colors. Semmes and half of his crew managed to escape on an English yacht.

In 1861, Southern officials had boasted of their many shore batteries and fortifications. But these seacoast strongholds proved to be no match for the heavy mobile firepower of the U.S. Navy. Federal ships applied pressure elsewhere by using rivers to penetrate deep into the heart of the South.

The Confederate navy had many daring officers and courageous sailors, but it never had enough strength to mount a serious challenge to the Union war fleets. Confederate naval activities were often spectacular, but it was the ever-tightening Union blockade of the South's 3,500 miles of coastline that led to final victory for the North.

Closing off the ports of the Confederacy had two major effects: first, it stopped the exportation of cotton that would have brought the South both money and a reputation as a stable country; and second, it stopped the importation of military supplies from abroad. From the very beginning of the war, the South found itself pinched and shut off from the rest of the world.

Slowly during the contest the U.S. Navy removed all threats on the waters. President Lincoln proudly stated late in the war: "Nor must Uncle Sam's web feet be forgotten. At all of the watery margins they have been present. Not only on the deep sea, the broad bay, the rapid river, but also up the narrow, muddy bayou, and wherever the ground was a little damp, they have been and made their mark."

Many foreigners watched from nearby sailboats as the CSS Alabama (FOREGROUND) *was sunk by the USS* Kearsarge *off the coast of France. (Battles and Leaders of the Civil War)*

10

1863: The Beginning of the End

As WINTER became spring in 1863, war exploded again. Grant's army began making its way slowly toward still-defiant Vicksburg, Mississippi. The opposing armies of Bragg and Rosecrans jabbed lightly at each other in middle Tennessee. In Virginia, the Federal Army of the Potomac started a campaign that might have won the Civil War but for the genius of Lee and the determination of his ragged band of veterans.

Federal general Joseph "Fighting Joe" Hooker had replaced Burnside that winter after the Union defeat at Fredericksburg, Virginia. Hooker was a hard-driving, hard-drinking officer who was popular with his men. He had spent the winter months building up both the strength and the morale of the North's major fighting machine. By April, the Army of the Potomac numbered 130,000 troops. It was "the finest army on the planet," Hooker boasted. Moreover, the battle plan that he adopted looked perfect—on paper.

Lee's poorly equipped force was encamped south of Fredericksburg and trying to recover from a severe winter. It numbered barely more than 50,000 soldiers because, several weeks earlier, Lee had detached Longstreet and 15,000 men to special duty in southeastern Virginia. Hooker had already determined before Longstreet's departure to take advantage of the huge Federal superiority in numbers by delivering attacks from three directions.

Federal cavalry would swoop around Lee's army and strike supply and communications lines between Lee and Richmond. About a third of Hooker's infantry would drive through Fredericksburg and attack Lee from the east. Hooker, with the other two-thirds of his army, would cross the Rappahannock several miles upriver and slam from the west into the other side of Lee's Confederates. The Southerners would be caught between the wings of the larger Federal army and squeezed into surrender.

It almost worked. Federal horsemen raced around Lee's flank but did little damage except to scare the citizens of Richmond. Hooker took his part of the Union forces up and across the Rappahannock. Union soldiers struggled through the area of dense trees and thick underbrush known as the Wilderness.

They were about to emerge from the dark woods when Hooker suddenly lost his confidence. To the disgust of his officers, the commander stopped the advance and ordered his thousands of troops to construct earthworks, or deep trenches, for defense. In that pause, and despite being so heavily outnumbered, Lee attacked on two fronts.

First, he sent 10,000 men to hold back the 40,000 Federals at Fredericksburg as long as possible. Next, Lee shifted the rest of his troops westward to confront Hooker's large wing. Finally, Lee sent two-thirds of the men he had left (28,000 soldiers under Jackson) on a twelve-mile circling march that would bring the Confederates into position on Hooker's unprotected flank.

It was the most dangerous gamble in Lee's military career. If either of the Federal forces drove between Lee's small and divided command, the Army of Northern Virginia—and the Confederacy—would be doomed.

Fighting Joe Hooker became commander of the Army of the Potomac in 1863. This 1862 photograph is here published for the first time. (Library of Congress)

Good luck and poor Union generalship worked in Lee's favor. Late in the afternoon of May 2, Stonewall Jackson's divisions came screaming through the tangled woods of the Wilderness and struck Hooker's line at Chancellorsville. The Confederates shattered a Federal corps of 12,000 men, then continued forward against other enemy units. Only darkness stopped the fighting. The next morning, Lee resumed the attacks. Hooker's lines slowly gave way as confusion reigned in the Federal army.

Lee clearly had control of the battle at Chancellorsville. He shook loose part of his forces and sent them back toward Fredericksburg to meet the other Union threat moving up behind him. At Salem Church, the Southerners fought the Federals to a standstill, then quickly rejoined Lee for another assault on Hooker's wing. The Federal commander had had enough. Hooker ordered his army (only a part of which had actually been engaged) back across the Rappahannock. The Chancellorsville campaign ended. Lee had won his greatest victory.

It came at a high price, however. Lee suffered more than 13,000 casualties. Among the slain was Stonewall Jackson, who died a week after accidentally being shot by his own men during the chaos of the first day's action. The death of Jackson sent shock waves throughout the South. As for Lee, who had considered Jackson his right arm, the loss was so great that never again would he attempt the surprise flank marches that Jackson had performed so brilliantly.

At Chancellorsville the Federal army lost a battle it should have won. The Army of the Potomac had again met defeat, at a cost of 17,000 of its soldiers and most of its morale.

Lee used the momentum gained at Chancellorsville to invade the North again, prompted by the desire for foreign assistance and the hope of forcing peace from the Union. More than half of Lee's 75,000 Confederates were barefooted, but they marched hard and with a sense of desperation.

The Southern army headed north through Pennsylvania. Two Confederate divisions left Lee's main body and turned east toward the little town of Gettysburg. It was an important road junction; it was also known to have a shoe factory.

On the outskirts of Gettysburg, the Confederates ran into Federal soldiers. They were the lead elements of the pursuing Army of the Potomac, now under the command of hot-tempered but dependable General George G. Meade. A. P. Hill's Confederate corps attacked in force. Fighting raged

This postwar painting by artist Warren B. Davis depicts Lee riding among his troops at the moment of victory at Chancellorsville. Burning in the background is the Chancellor family mansion, around which much of the battle raged. (The Bettmann Archive)

throughout the day. By nightfall the outnumbered Federals had fallen back to a range of hills south of town.

Confederate general Richard Stoddert Ewell had recently been promoted to take command of most of Jackson's old corps. Ewell was a brave officer who had lost a leg in battle the year before. He was unsure of himself at Gettysburg. His failure to drive the Federals from the ridges south of town proved to be a critical factor in the outcome of the battle. Another Confederate failing was the absence of Jeb Stuart's Southern cavalry. Stuart was spending too much time raiding through Pennsylvania and not enough time supplying badly needed information on Federal troop movements.

For the next two days, Lee delivered assault after assault against the ever-strengthening Union lines. The climax came on the extremely hot afternoon of July 3. Lee sent two divisions under General George Edward Pickett in a frontal attack against the center of the Union position.

Some 15,000 Confederates advanced across 400 yards of open ground and in clear view of the entrenched Federal soldiers. "Pickett's Charge" looked like a parade. Men were in precise lines and marching steadily; color-bearers proudly waved regimental flags; officers moved back and forth in front of the ranks as they led troops forward.

Union cannoneers and infantrymen opened concentrated fire. The at-

tack slowly fell apart as artillery shells blew large gaps in the Southern ranks and Federal musketry sent Confederates slumping to the ground by the thousands. Barely half of the attackers made it back to their lines. With that final repulse, the three-day nightmare at Gettysburg ended.

Both armies had taken dreadful losses. Meade's 23,049 casualties included 3,155 killed. One-third of Lee's army had been slain or wounded. His 22,200 killed, wounded, and captured included seventeen of the fifty-two generals in that Confederate army.

On the Fourth of July, with the dead unburied, what was left of Lee's army limped southward through heavy rain. Meade's army was too bloodied and weary to make more than a weak effort to catch Lee. Nevertheless, the Army of the Potomac had at last won a victory against Lee. The Confederate army recrossed the Potomac into Virginia. It was the last time the Army of Northern Virginia would ever see the river dividing North from South.

This rare photograph of troops in actual combat shows men of the 2nd U.S. Artillery loading their guns near Fredericksburg, Virginia, in the spring of 1863. (Library of Congress)

Meade's Federals marched slowly back into Virginia. For the remainder of 1863, the two opposing armies maneuvered back and forth between Alexandria and Culpeper as each tried unsuccessfully to outflank or overwhelm the other. Federal victory in a brief fight at Bristoe Station and sharp skirmishes at Mine Run were bloody but indecisive affairs. The July fighting in Pennsylvania proved to be the last major battle in the eastern theater that year.

At about the same moment that the Federals stopped Lee at Gettysburg, their western forces won an even more spectacular triumph. Grant spent most of the spring of that year placing his troops on the high dry ground east of the Mississippi River in position to attack the heavily fortified Confederate position at Vicksburg, Mississippi. On the other side of the Mississippi were bayous and swamps that blocked all approaches to Vicksburg from that direction.

In March, Federal ships under Admiral David D. Porter steamed under fire past Vicksburg and took control of much of the river south of the city. Grant marched his troops down the west side of the river and joined with the fleet below Vicksburg. He ferried his men across the Mississippi and demonstrated the same boldness that Lee had shown in Virginia. Grant cut away from his supply bases and led his army into Mississippi proper. His first objective was to capture the state capital at Jackson.

The Confederates should have brought their forces together to block Grant's approach. Instead, under orders from President Davis, they remained isolated in the various river forts. Grant fought his way to victories at Port Gibson and Raymond before capturing Jackson itself. This cut off Vicksburg from the rest of the Confederacy. Grant then moved swiftly back to the Mississippi River. On May 16, his army won a hard-fought victory at Champion's Hill. This success drove the Confederates into their main defensive works at Vicksburg.

Grant curled his army around the northern, eastern, and southern sides of the town. On May 22, a grand assault by three full corps failed and cost the Union army 3,000 men killed and wounded. This setback made Grant decide to strangle Vicksburg into surrender through siege operations. Federals would surround the town, cut off all supplies, and wait for the defenders to give up from hunger and want.

For the next forty-seven days, Grant's 70,000 troops occupied a fifteen-mile line two trenches deep around the trapped city. Both Federal flanks were on the Mississippi. The river itself was Grant's supply line. The determined Federal general was in a position that no Confederate force in the West could break.

Inside Vicksburg were 28,000 Confederate soldiers as well as the city's residents. All had to take refuge in basements and hillside caves to survive the daily artillery bombardments. Starvation became widespread. A Confederate soldier inside Vicksburg wrote in his diary that the men had eaten everything they had: "all the beef—all the mules—all the Dogs—all the Rats."

On July 4, the weary Confederates surrendered Vicksburg. Grant agreed that the Southern soldiers would be paroled—set free on the promise that they would not fight again—rather than be locked in prisoner-of-war camps. Five days later, a second Federal force accepted the surrender of the equally ragged Confederate garrison at Port Hudson, Louisiana. Grant's triumph in the long Vicksburg campaign was one of the most brilliant of the war. He had inflicted 10,000 casualties, captured 37,000 Southerners (including fifteen generals), and seized 60,000 rifles and 172 cannon—all at a cost of 9,000 men killed and wounded.

Grant's success at Vicksburg cut off the trans-Mississippi from the rest of the Confederacy. More importantly, a happy Lincoln exclaimed, "The Father of Waters [the Mississippi River] again goes unvexed to the sea." The river was now totally in Federal hands. Vicksburg and Gettysburg, occurring at the same time, sent sadness and fear across the South.

A third major campaign in 1863 was the bitter contest in the western theater for control of middle and eastern Tennessee. For five months after the battle of Murfreesboro, the armies of Bragg and Rosecrans faced each other in the rolling country south of Nashville. Each was hesitant to attack the other. While the infantry watched and waited, Confederate cavalry swept back and forth across Tennessee. The exploits of General Bedford Forrest and his horsemen were especially noteworthy.

Victories at Thompson's Station, Brentwood, and Franklin, plus a spectacular running fight with Federal cavalry through Alabama and into Georgia, established Forrest as the finest cavalry commander in the war. But both sides knew it was the infantry that would decide the outcome of the struggle. As a result, attention focused on Rosecrans's 63,000 and Bragg's 45,000 foot soldiers.

Rosecrans moved forward in late June. By a series of skillful marches and maneuvers in constant rain, the Federal general drove Bragg from his base of supplies at Tullahoma, Tennessee. The Confederates retreated southeast to the more important supply depot and rail junction at Chattanooga. There Bragg dug in to await the next Federal move.

It came in September. Bragg expected Rosecrans's army to come from the west. To his surprise, Federal forces appeared to the south of Chattanooga. Rosecrans was about to march around the Confederates and cut the Western & Atlantic Railroad. The rail line was Bragg's only way of communicating with Atlanta and the Deep South. Bragg abandoned Chattanooga and fell back into Georgia. As he did so, he gathered reinforcements and made plans to attack the badly divided Federals. However, Rosecrans managed to get his army together just before Bragg struck.

The September 19–20 battle raged along a little stream that Indians had named Chickamauga centuries earlier. The word means "River of Death," and death swept over that region as Bragg's troops charged the Federal positions in what became the bloodiest two-day engagement of the Civil War.

Confederates attacked repeatedly. However, the charges were scattered and lacked the punching power necessary to break through the Federal breastworks of logs and earth. (Breastworks were so-named because they were chest-high.) Fighting was desperate. On the second day of action, the fresh corps of Confederate general James Longstreet arrived on the field from Virginia. It slammed into the right-center of Rosecrans's position.

The attack came just as a division of Union troops had pulled out of that sector to strengthen the Union left. No other troops took their place in the line. By sheer luck, Longstreet's Confederates drove straight through the gap.

Two of Rosecrans's six divisions became what a Union observer called a "panic-stricken rabble." Thousands of Federals ran pell-mell toward Chattanooga. Meanwhile, part of the Union army held firm at Chickamauga. The Federal commander of that sector, General George H. Thomas, drew back his flanks and formed a horseshoe-shaped line. For the rest of the day, Union soldiers held their ground against strong assaults. Thomas saved the Union army. Thereafter he was known as the "Rock of Chickamauga."

With the Confederates in control of most of the battlefield, the South had won a victory. That victory would have been even greater if Bragg had launched new attacks against the splintered Federal army, but the Confederate general was too shocked by his losses to realize how successful his troops had been in the battle.

A third of the Confederate Army of Tennessee was dead, wounded, or missing. Rosecrans likewise had lost a third of his forces. The two armies together suffered 35,000 casualties in a battle that achieved little for either side except to cast doubts on the real ability of both Bragg and Rosecrans.

Fragments of the Union army fell back and occupied Chattanooga. Bragg moved forward cautiously and took position on the high hills overlooking the city from the south and east. The Confederate plan was to lay siege to Chattanooga and force Rosecrans's army to surrender.

Fortunately for Rosecrans's army, Bragg's "siege" was not effective. By November, men and supplies in great quantities were inside Chattanooga. So was General Grant, who arrived and took overall command of Federal operations.

Bragg helped the Federal cause by scattering his own meager forces. He sent Longstreet's corps to Knoxville in what proved to be a long and empty siege of that important town. Accompanying Longstreet was most of the Confederate cavalry. Bragg was looking down on Chattanooga from Lookout Mountain and Missionary Ridge with barely half of his army.

On the morning of November 24, clouds covered the hilltops and a heavy mist hung in the air. Union troops fought their way up the steep face of Lookout Mountain. The "Battle Above the Clouds" resulted in the Federals' driving Bragg's defenders from that point. Other Union troops moved to the base of nearby Missionary Ridge.

The following day, Grant ordered part of the Union army to advance a short distance up Missionary Ridge. Federals moved up the hill and overran the first Confederate line. Without orders, and in an assault as gallant as Pickett's Confederate charge at Gettysburg, the Union soldiers continued scrambling up the rocky hillside under heavy fire. Shouts of victory echoed across the valley as Federal troops broke through the center of the Confederate line. The once-proud Army of Tennessee fell apart.

Under cover of a chilly darkness, the Confederates retreated toward Georgia. Tennessee had been one of the Confederacy's most important states. Now the greater part of it was under Federal occupation. U. S. Grant had ended the year as the man of the hour in the North.

Gettysburg, Vicksburg, Chattanooga—all had been crippling defeats for the Southern nation in 1863. Thousands of miles of territory had fallen to the Federals, including the trans-Mississippi, Louisiana, Arkansas, Mississippi, and Tennessee. Confederate armies were battered, ragged, and dangerously ill-equipped. Union forces seemed to be growing stronger each week, and President Lincoln was determined to press the war to Northern victory.

Late in November, Lincoln went to Gettysburg for the dedication of a national cemetery for many of the men who were killed there four months earlier. He was not the main speaker at the ceremonies; he had been invited out of courtesy to make "a few appropriate remarks."

This he did. His Gettysburg Address was comprised of only 267 words. Its beautiful phrases gave comfort to the North, and the closing statement became a timeless call to duty: "It is rather for us to be here dedicated to the great task remaining before us—that from these honored dead we take increased devotion to that cause for which they gave the last full measure of devotion—that we here highly resolve that these dead shall not have died in vain—that this nation, under God, shall have a new birth of freedom—and that government of the people, by the people, for the people, shall not perish from the earth."

This is the earliest known copy of the Gettysburg Address, which Lincoln wrote himself on White House stationery. A few word changes were made in later versions. (R. R. Donnelley & Sons, Inc.)

11

Johnny Rebs and Billy Yanks

THE YOUNGEST Civil War soldier was a nine-year-old lad from Mississippi. The oldest was an eighty-year-old great-grandfather from Iowa. One of every four men who served in the Union armies was Irish, Norwegian, German, French, or some other nationality. They had come to America in the late 1840s and 1850s in search of a new and better life.

Farm boys, students, merchants, blacksmiths, and clerks were the backbone of the Civil War armies. Every occupation, age, shape, and size could be found among the three million Americans who wore the blue of the North and the gray of the South.

Early in the war, soldiers on each side became known by common nicknames. People in the North, especially in New England, had been called Yankees ever since the days when they were colonists. It therefore became natural for the Federal soldiers of the Civil War to be called Yanks.

Many people thought that the Southern Confederacy was waging a rebellion. Hence, Southern troops were known as Rebs. As months passed, and for no real reason, soldiers came to refer to themselves and the other side as "Billy Yanks" and "Johnny Rebs."

They were products of a simpler time, and they possessed an enthusiasm for life that was a reflection of America's growth in the mid-nineteenth century. The Northerners and Southerners who rushed to enlist in 1861 and 1862 did so with a feeling of excitement and youthful innocence. Less than a week after the conflict began, an Ohio student wrote: "War! and volunteers are the only topic of conversation or thought. The lessons today

LEFT: *This Union infantryman, not in full uniform, stands with a Bowie knife as his only weapon. (National Archives)*

BELOW: *David Wood, a ten-year-old Union drummer boy, dressed in an officer's coat and holding a borrowed revolver. (Private collection)*

BOTTOM: *Three members of a Georgia regiment. (Museum of the Confederacy)*

have been a mere form. I cannot study. I cannot sleep. I cannot work, and I don't know as I can write." Just a few days later, far to the south, Governor John Pettus sent a telegram to President Davis: "All Mississippi is in a fever to [leave for war], and hail an order to march as the greatest favor you can confer upon them."

Army life then was a far cry from what it is now. Civil War troops quickly lost their enthusiasm and pleasure when they encountered the painful shock of camp. Equipment and training were unusually poor; food, quarters, and medical attention were even worse.

Many officers did not know much more than the soldiers about how to live in tents and how to fight in battle. In the first months of the war, whenever an alarm would sound in the camp of one Virginia regiment, all that its colonel knew to shout was: "Attention, my people! Fall in! Them fellows air a-coming!"

Johnny Rebs and Billy Yanks were "citizens in arms" more than they were soldiers, because most of them never fully accepted the blind obedience and strict devotion to duty that true soldier life requires. However, they were warlike in nature—possessing the traditional American trait of reacting sharply to insults and threats. The men of blue and gray may not have been the best of soldiers, but because of their courage and determination in the face of bloody battles and severe suffering, historians such as Bell I. Wiley and David Donald have ranked them as the greatest fighting men of all time.

Their gallantry becomes more outstanding when we remember that these men lived in the wrong place at the wrong time. Northern and Southern boys went into the armies just as a whole series of new weapons was making killing easier and, therefore, more widespread. Furthermore, in the 1860s little was known about treating wounds and fighting disease.

In other words, when 50,000 to 100,000 soldiers came together into an army, they lived in conditions that made them sick. When they went into combat in such large numbers, they were likely to be hurt very badly. And they had little or no chance of receiving the medical treatment that we take for granted today.

Under the circumstances, Johnny Rebs and Billy Yanks endured as best they could. Many soldiers were well educated and came from comfortable backgrounds; others were extremely poor and unable to either read or write. The typical Civil War soldier was a farmer, unmarried, and about twenty-one years old. He had had two to three years of formal education. His writing was very crude, and he tended to spell words phonetically—that is, the way he spoke them. In letters home many men would write "git" for "get," "thar" for "there," "bin" for "been," "wuz" for "was," "yestiddy" for "yesterday," and the like. Few soldiers paid attention to periods, commas, and capital letters. They also wrote as they thought, so that sentences tumbled forth with little connection to one another.

Joining the army often marked the first time that Northern and Southern boys had ever been away from home. It did not take long for the early excitement of army life to vanish. There were no radios, telephones, movies, or television; newspapers and magazines were quite scarce. Little existed to keep the soldiers' minds occupied. The result was that the men in camp were soon deeply homesick. "I never knew how to value home until I came into the army," a North Carolinian wrote his loved ones. An Indiana soldier said the same thing to his parents: "When i lay Down at night, i think of home, But it dont do eny good."

The only contact with loved ones hundreds of miles behind the lines was by mail—which is why more letter writing took place in the Civil War than at any other time in American history. "I never thought so much of letters as I have since I have been here," a Pennsylvania recruit wrote from camp in 1862. A year later, a Connecticut soldier told his sweetheart: "The soldier looks upon a letter from home as a perfect God send—sent as it were, by some kind ministering Angel Spirit, to cheer his dark and weary hours."

The overwhelming number of soldiers in the armies of North and South were sentimental. They spent much of every letter expressing love for family and friends left behind, and hopes that the war would soon end so that all could be together again. Often, in love letters to a wife or a sweetheart, a soldier would try his hand at poetry. One popular couplet ran:

> My pen is poor my ink is pale
> My love for you shall never fail.

A few soldiers became quite good at writing in rhyme. Private W. A. Roberts of Alabama began an 1863 letter to his wife with a poem that closed with the lines:

Union soldiers reading letters and playing cards to pass the time during the siege of Petersburg, Virginia. (National Archives)

> When heart to heart we plighted love
> Affection's tender vow
> I loved thee then my Mary Dear
> But love thee better now.

Soldiers wrote about anything and everything. John Shank, a poorly educated Illinois private, once began a letter home with the statement: "They is a fly on my pen. I just rights What ever Comes in my head." Men expressed strong opinions about all aspects of army life, and they voiced those opinions freely in their letters and diaries.

Officers were always a target for criticism. An Alabama private wrote his wife that "Gen. Jones is a very common looking man who rides [a horse] just like he had a boil on his stern." George Hunter of Pennsylvania observed on one occasion: "I am well convinced in My own Mind that had it not been for officers this war would have Ended long ago." A truly biting comment came from an Illinois soldier, who stated in anger: "I wish to God one half of our officers were knocked in the head by slinging them Against A part of those still left."

The troops complained about having to march and drill so much, especially since they generally did so in stifling heat and choking dust—or in cold rain and deep mud. The drills themselves seemed like foolishness to many. A New Hampshire Yank watched his regiment go through the various steps and lunges of bayonet drill. He concluded that the men looked "like a line of beings made up about equally of the frog, the sand-hill crane, the sentinel crab, and the grasshopper; all of them rapidly jumping, thrusting, swinging, striking, jerking every which way, and all gone stark mad."

Soldiers viewed life inside a tent as more like life inside a pigpen. Six men usually slept in tents designed for only four. A smaller, two-man tent introduced in 1862 quickly became known as a "dog shanty" or "pup tent" because, as one Federal believed, "it would only comfortably accommodate a dog, and a small one at that."

Civil War troops often found that army food either did not exist or was unfit to eat. Men encamped in one place for any length of time received army rations on a regular basis, but those on the march or engaged in battle often went hungry for days. Many soldiers were not sure whether it was better to endure the pain of an empty stomach or to eat the horrible food they received.

The meat distributed to regiments was old, salted, or pickled. Whichever way, it was not tasty. Soldiers called their meat rations "salt horse," "sowbelly," and other pointed names. Sometimes the meat was rotting. One Billy Yank with imagination stated: "Yesterday morning was the first time we had to carry our meat for the maggots [fly larvae] always carried it until then. We had to have an extra gard to keep them from packing it clear off."

Nor was the bread ration any better. Confederates received coarse cornmeal that soldiers fried in the shape of large cakes, or pones. The cooked black pones did not look appealing, and the rough cornmeal was difficult to digest. For Union troops, the standard bread ration was a large cracker known as hardtack. Almost without exception, the crackers were so stale and hard that they could not be chewed. The men referred to hardtack as "sheet iron crackers" and "teeth dullers."

To the troops of the 1860s, an individual's religion was a personal and important matter. Each man expressed himself as he felt best. Sometimes their prayers were informal—and a bit humorous. Once, just as a battle was starting, a Confederate offered this last-minute plea: "Lord, if you ain't for us, don't be agin us. Just step aside and watch one of the worst fights you are ever likely to see!"

Army chaplains, although few in number, labored long and hard to meet the religious needs of the men. Crudely built churches quickly appeared whenever an army camped for several days. Formal services and prayer meetings were common sights in the Union and Confederate armies. Countless soldiers kept their deep faith to the end of their lives. After one of the battles fought near Richmond, Virginia, a burial detail found a dead Southerner lying on the field. His hand lay on a Bible. It was open at the Twenty-third Psalm and the words "Thy rod and Thy staff, they comfort me."

The most important test of any soldier comes in battle. The Civil War was no exception. As untested men prepared for their first combat, their deepest fear was not of being wounded. Many of them hoped that they might get a "red badge of courage," so long as it was not a serious wound.

What the average soldier dreaded almost as much as death was cowardice—"showing the white feather" in the face of the enemy. As a Connecticut recruit told his parents in an 1862 letter: "I hope as I always have, that I may have the courage to do my duty well, not recklessly but with simple bravery and fidelity, so that if I fall you may have the consolation of knowing that I not only lose my life in a good cause but die like a man."

In every battle there was human leakage: men who could stand some things but not everything. Yet for every soldier who lacked courage, Northern as well as Southern, a hundred or more rose to the heights of heroism.

When an artillery shell tore both hands off a Kentucky soldier, the man stared numbly at his two bleeding stumps and mumbled only: "My Lord, that stops my fighting." In another battle, an officer was walking across a field covered with bodies. Suddenly he heard a feeble call. It came from a dying soldier in his regiment. "Colonel," the soldier asked with pain, "is the day ours?"

"Yes," the colonel said. "The day is ours. We are victorious."

"Then," the young private replied, "I am willing to die."

And he did die. The soldier lies buried today on the battlefield where

he gave his life. Johnny Rebs and Billy Yanks left a rich heritage to the nation. Their devotion to their causes, and their sacrifice of themselves, are lasting symbols that the real strength of the United States forever rests with its plain people.

12

Blacks and the Door to Freedom

THE CIVIL WAR was a chain-breaking revolution for blacks, North and South. The struggle that created a permanent union also brought freedom and the promise of citizenship and equality to all black people in this country. For them, the journey to freedom was filled with roadblocks—sometimes dangerous, always painful.

Slavery was the backbone of antebellum Southern life. Secession and the possibility of war only strengthened Southern determination to maintain the slave system. As Confederate vice president Alexander Stephens proclaimed in March 1861: "Our confederacy is founded upon . . . the great truth that the negro is not equal to the white man. That slavery—subordination to the superior race, is his natural and normal condition."

War with the North raised an entirely new set of problems for Southern slaveholders. White males were needed for the armies. The Confederacy had to devote its energies to mobilizing against a much larger enemy while keeping three and a half million slaves housed, fed, and busy at the same time. The slaves also had to be watched, or they might use the confusion of war to run away or band together and start uprisings of their own.

No major slave revolts took place in the wartime South. Many slaves were afraid to undertake any kind of rebellion. Others remained loyal servants throughout the war. Large numbers simply waited to see what would happen in the contest between Union and Confederacy.

The loyalty of a Southern slave depended primarily on the kind of plantation work he performed, the kindness of his owner, and the closeness of Union troops. A field hand who had little personal contact with the master was more likely to run away than a household servant treated like a member of the white family. Cold-hearted masters and cruel overseers could not expect a slave to remain blindly loyal when the opportunity to escape arose. As invading Federal forces moved through the South from Virginia to Missouri, thousands of unhappy slaves rushed to freedom inside army lines.

During the war, Confederate and Southern state governments used slaves in many different ways. Some blacks drove supply wagons or served as cooks in the Confederate armies. Others acted as stretcher-bearers, ambulance drivers, and hospital attendants. Even greater numbers of slaves were forced to work on the South's railroads, where the heavy demands of war kept the lines in constant need of repair.

Other slaves labored in various Confederate industries, such as the Tredegar Iron Works in Richmond, Virginia. Blacks built gun emplacements and dug earthworks around major Southern cities threatened by Federal armies. The Confederacy would have been much weaker against Union attacks but for the wartime labor performed by slaves.

Throughout the war the Southern government wrestled with the question of whether or not to use slaves as soldiers. Black freedmen and slaves had fought as volunteers against the French and Indians as well as in the American Revolution and the War of 1812. In none of those conflicts were they officially accepted as U.S. soldiers. Blacks had served when needed; when the particular crisis ended, they became freedmen and slaves again. A 1792 federal law even prohibited blacks from joining state militia units.

Confederate leaders warned repeatedly that putting weapons into the hands of hundreds of slaves would create an uncontrollable danger to helpless white Southerners. Other defenders of slavery in the wartime South voiced an even deeper concern. If black men went into the Confederate army and fought well, the long-held belief that blacks were inferior to whites would be destroyed. A Georgia senator put it bluntly: "The day you make soldiers of them is the end of [our] revolution. If slaves will make good soldiers, our whole theory of slavery is wrong."

Not until March 1865, with the war all but lost, did the Confederacy finally let wartime need take precedence over personal safety and pride. Authorities in Richmond approved the creation of two black regiments, but the Civil War ended before those units could get to the front lines.

Blacks who fled into Union lines in 1861 and 1862 had escaped from slavery, but they had not secured freedom. By law they were contraband—enemy war matériel that the Federals had seized. The best way for those former slaves to win acceptance in American society was to prove themselves worthy in battle. Yet blacks had to fight for the right to fight before they could fight for freedom.

In the first two years of the Civil War, strong and widespread opposition prevailed in the North against using blacks as soldiers. The majority of Northern leaders looked on blacks as the race that had caused the war by their presence. They were inferior beings; they could not fight in battle; whites did not want to serve in the armies with them.

One Federal general stated in 1862: "I cannot bring myself to trust Negroes with arms in positions of danger and trust." Another Union official thought the idea of arming slaves to be "more productive of evil than good."

Large numbers of freed blacks assisted the Union army by serving as wagon drivers, laborers, and—as in this photograph—dockworkers. (The Bettmann Archive)

Antiblack feelings throughout the North began to melt in the late summer of 1862. Battle casualties had taken a heavy toll, and many soldiers were at the end of their one-year term of enlistment. Men were badly needed for the Union armies. That need, coupled with louder demands from abolitionists, free blacks, and escaped slaves, brought a change in thinking among key Federal leaders.

President Lincoln began to see the value of using blacks in the army. Several of Lincoln's cabinet members felt that the Emancipation Proclamation should be more than an announcement that all slaves in the Confederate States would be free. The proclamation could become a recruiting tool for enlisting black soldiers.

Enrollment of blacks began in the first months of 1863. A few units comprised of runaways and Southern freedmen were accepted into military service. A larger boost to the black-soldier program came with the March 1863 conscription act. That law subjected white Northerners to being conscripted, or drafted, into the armies.

Conscription brought a quick change of mind to thousands of Union citizens who had previously opposed using blacks as soldiers. Whites now subject to the draft began to think that a black could "stop a bullet as well as any man." Lincoln felt differently. To a Northern governor he wrote: "The bare sight of 50,000 armed and drilled black soldiers . . . would end the rebellion at once. And who doubts that we can present that sight, if we but take hold in earnest?"

Enlistment efforts intensified in the occupied South and throughout the North. The most successful recruiter was the North's adjutant general, Lorenzo Thomas. A hardworking officer with no experience in field command, Thomas traveled up and down the Mississippi Valley enlisting exslaves and freedmen as soldiers. The general did an equally good job in persuading many battle-hardened white Billy Yanks to accept blacks as soldiers. All told, Thomas raised 76,000 black troops, nearly half the total number of blacks in the Union armies.

But neither Thomas nor any other individual could stop the constant discrimination against black soldiers during the Civil War. Almost all of them were placed in the infantry rather than the more colorful artillery and cavalry units. They served in separate all-black regiments and, with few exceptions, all of the officers in black regiments were white.

Federal officials justified this policy on the grounds that blacks were too lacking in military experience to make good officers. The white-officer practice was eventually abandoned, but fewer than a hundred blacks obtained officer commissions. No black rose above the rank of captain.

"Colored troops," as they were officially called, received only half as much pay as whites. Black soldiers were usually assigned the worst army duties—cleaning out latrines, digging earthworks, policing camps, performing long hours of guard duty. They were given the worst arms and the most inferior equipment available. Northern white soldiers bullied them, beat them, and sometimes even shot them.

The discrimination did not stop there. Confederate authorities regarded uniformed blacks as runaway slaves, not as soldiers protected by the rules of war. Captured black troops were not always treated as pris-

oners of war. Some were sold back into slavery. Others were executed.

Assigning black soldiers to filthy camp duties not only increased their chances of becoming sick; the degrading work further strengthened the idea of their inferiority as a race. Colonels of black regiments, abolitionists, and freed black leaders all pleaded with the federal government to send blacks into battle so that they could prove themselves as trustworthy men.

Frederick Douglass, the most prominent black spokesman of the Civil War period, told a Northern audience in the spring of 1863 that black soldiers deserved the opportunity to defend the Union in combat. "I don't

A guard detail of the 107th U.S. Colored Troops at a fort near Washington, D.C. (Library of Congress)

In battle after battle, beginning in 1863, black men fought their way to glory as well as respect. (Harper's Weekly)

say that they will fight better than other men," Douglass exclaimed. "All I say is, give them a chance!"

That chance came in May 1863 at Port Hudson, Louisiana. Two black regiments attacked a strongly fortified Confederate position. The blacks were repulsed with heavy losses, but their courage impressed one and all. Ten days after Port Hudson, black soldiers beat back a Southern assault at Milliken's Bend, Louisiana. However, it was at Fort Wagner, South Carolina, that glory came to black Billy Yanks.

The 54th Massachusetts was the first black regiment organized in the North. It was the Union's showcase unit—a regiment that would display black soldiers at their best. Freed blacks filled the ranks of the 54th Massachusetts. The men wore spotless uniforms and carried new weapons. Commanding the regiment was Colonel Robert Gould Shaw, the son of a prominent Boston family.

Seven weeks after leaving Boston, the new unit received orders to participate in an attack on Fort Wagner, a Confederate earthen fort guarding the entrance to the Charleston, South Carolina, harbor. It was one of the strongest points in the Confederate defenses.

Just getting into position for the assault was a terrible ordeal for the 54th Massachusetts. On July 17, 1863, the troops struggled through a marshland in pouring rain. The following day, they trudged six miles through sand and under a boiling sun. It was almost sunset when they reached the area where they—along with six white regiments—were to attack.

The 54th Massachusetts had been two nights without rest and two days without food when the signal came to advance. Black soldiers fought their way into part of the enemy works, held on briefly, but had to fall back in the face of heavy gunfire. More than 350 blacks were killed, wounded, or captured. Colonel Shaw was also slain in the battle.

A Federal officer who watched that July 18 charge across the open beach stated that "language is all too tame to convey the horrors and meaning of it all." The Federal lines were blasted to pieces by concentrated fire from the Southerners. It was a stunning Union defeat. Yet the 54th Massachusetts had proved its ability to fight and die for the Union cause. Historian Allan Nevins concluded: "All colored Americans stood on higher ground after Fort Wagner."

Black soldiers were in the field for only two years during the Civil War, but they participated in thirty-nine different engagements. Of the 179,000 blacks who served in the U.S. Army, about 2,800 were killed in action; more than 65,000 blacks died from sickness and disease.

Suffering did not dampen their spirits. From a hospital bed one black soldier, who had lost an arm in battle, expressed feelings shared by the ex-slaves and freedmen who had served with him. "Well," he said, " 'twas lost in a glorious cause, and if I'd lost my life I should have been satisfied. I knew what I was fighting for."

A final and fitting tribute to black soldiers came in the spring of 1865. Selected to lead President Lincoln's funeral procession were the men of the 22nd U.S. Colored Troops.

13

Diseases, Wounds, and Death

SICKNESS WAS the biggest killer in the Civil War. Some 400,000 of the 600,000 Johnny Rebs and Billy Yanks who died were victims of germs rather than bullets. Put another way: for every man killed in battle, two died behind the lines from some form of illness. Fully half of a Civil War army was "absent sick" at any given time.

There were a number of reasons for so much sickness and suffering in the 1860s. In the first stages of the Civil War, almost anyone who could stand on two feet was permitted to enlist. If a man was doing well in a civilian job, he was considered fit for military duty. Thousands of recruits entered the army when they should not have been accepted. A Union inspector wrote in 1862 that "at least twenty-five percent of the army raised last year" was "utterly worthless."

Most Civil War soldiers were farm boys who had never had any serious diseases. Once they entered the army camps, sickness of every kind descended on them. These plagues struck the troops in two waves. First were the so-called childhood epidemics—chicken pox, smallpox, mumps, and especially measles. Such diseases did not always kill a soldier, but they sometimes left him so weak that he became easy prey for more serious illnesses.

The second wave of sicknesses were "camp diseases"—typhoid fever, diarrhea, dysentery, yellow fever, and malaria. Bad drinking water, poor food, inadequate clothing, and mosquitoes were the principal causes.

Whatever the disease, the army physician had no cure. He simply made the patient as comfortable as he could while the illness ran its course. Without proper medicine, typhoid fever, malaria, and chronic dysentery were usually fatal.

Intestinal disorders in the form of excessive bowel movements were most common. "No matter what else a patient had," one hospital surgeon observed, "he had diarrhea." This ailment alone claimed more victims than any other, including the enemy. When a soldier could not control his body functions, he lost the desire for food and then the will to live. At that time physicians did not know how to relieve such disorders. Soldiers struck down by diarrhea either became well by themselves or slowly and painfully died from weakness and loss of blood and body fluids.

Exposure to bad weather, particularly in winter, led to much suffering. After the first few months of army life, thousands of Confederates had worn out the only shoes they owned. Many soldiers on both sides lacked raincoats and even blankets. They lived and slept in rain, sleet, and snow with little or no protection.

During Virginia's bitterly cold winter of 1862–1863, a New Hampshire soldier wrote: "It is fearful to wake at night, and to hear the sounds made by the men about you. All night long the sounds go up of men coughing, breathing heavy and hoarse with half-choked throats, moaning and groaning with acute pain." Untold numbers of men froze to death while huddled around little campfires.

Homesickness added to the danger of any disease. The majority of Civil War soldiers were away from home for the first time in their lives. The more lonely they were, the weaker they became. When a homesick boy fell ill, he often did not have the strength to fight his illness.

Rotten food always brought a new outbreak of diarrhea. In the Southern armies, many men lived for months on nothing but greasy bits of meat and coarse fried cornbread. Because farmhands were few, fields lay idle, and with supply lines cut, fresh vegetables were rarely available. This scarcity caused the dread disease known as scurvy to strike army camps many times.

Water in a soldier's canteen came from wherever he could find it. A camp reporter once noted that the water in the area smelled so bad "that the men have to hold their noses while drinking it." Foul water led directly to typhoid fever. In several regiments that had seen many battles, typhoid fever killed more soldiers than did the enemy.

Army camps were filthy beyond description. Soldiers were supposed to take a complete bath once a week. Most troops went for months without bathing because of laziness, lack of soap, dirty water, and no change of clothing. What they were wearing was all that they owned. The lack of hygiene attracted hordes of flies, mosquitoes, lice, and fleas. They in turn brought new diseases and more suffering.

Once a soldier became sick, he could not expect to get much medical treatment. Although army medical men of the Civil War were called surgeons, only a few of them actually performed operations. The typical surgeon examined patients and distributed what medicines he had. Army physicians were few in number. On average, there was one Union surgeon for every 133 men and one Confederate physician for every 324 men.

Even worse was the level of medical knowledge during the Civil War. In those days, most physicians received their training by working with another doctor for a while or by attending medical school for two years. Since at least 90 percent of present-day medicine was not known in the Civil War years, it did not take long to acquire a "medical education."

Such things as blood transfusions, x-rays, antibiotics, vitamins, and vaccinations for anything but smallpox lay in the future. So did such treatment as setting a broken bone. Civil War surgeons might cut off an arm or a leg, but they never operated on the body. That was regarded as barbaric.

Worst of all in the treatments of the 1860s was an ignorance of germs. Most physicians dismissed the idea that unseen little objects could produce sickness. No more than half a dozen microscopes existed in the United States at the time of the Civil War.

Medical treatment was a mixture of guesswork and superstition. Many "remedies" had been handed down through the doctor's family or were taken from almanacs and similar sources. For example, when a patient was suffering from heart failure or a concussion, physicians would pour boiling water on the chest or head to drive the "evil spirits" from the area in question. Civil War surgeons were also convinced that a wound giving off vile-smelling pus was actually a sign of healing. Therefore, they worked hard at keeping the wound oozing—even to the extent of ripping off scabs when they formed.

Confusion and lack of knowledge were the basic qualities of Civil War medicine. This was especially true with cases involving battle wounds.

In Vietnam, only one of every 200 American GIs who fell wounded

Kneeling surgeons try to treat dozens of sick and wounded men during the 1862 Peninsular Campaign. (Battles and Leaders of the Civil War)

ultimately died. In the Civil War, that ratio was one of every four soldiers. Why the odds of surviving in the 1860s were so small can best be seen by following a wounded soldier from the battlefield.

Many of the wounded had to make their own way to the field hospital in the rear or be carried by friends. The "lucky" ones were placed in an ambulance—a wagon without springs, cots, or mattresses. Bleeding and mangled soldiers found themselves tossed back and forth as the wagon bounced along the road. It was easy to identify ambulance wagons by the screams that came from within.

Field hospitals were located a mile or so behind the battle lines. The hospital might be a clearing, a clump of woods, a church, a barn, or some farmer's front yard. Wherever it was, the field hospital was something no wounded soldier ever forgot. Hundreds of men, with every possible kind of injury, lay sprawled on the ground. Nearby, one or two surgeons worked as fast as they could while the waiting lines grew longer.

The operating table was usually a wooden door or several boards laid on top of two barrels. Sanitation was little more than an idea in the minds of some physicians. Army surgeons, their shirt sleeves rolled up and their aprons covered with blood, probed wounds with ungloved fingers. Some

On the hills behind this field hospital are columns of advancing soldiers and the smoke of battle. Other troops (RIGHT), waiting to move into action, watch with horror as surgeons drag a thrashing soldier onto an operating table. (Harper's Weekly)

sharpened their scalpels on the soles of their shoes. They would take blood-soaked, germ-infected bandages off a dead soldier and use the same bandages on the next wounded man.

Nothing could be done about the thousands of flies and gnats that swarmed around the area and covered those wounded men too weak to swat them away.

The primary work of the surgeons was the treatment of bullet wounds. Musket balls of the Civil War were made of soft lead. The heat of the exploding gunpowder behind the bullets made them even softer, so that they lost their shape as soon as they struck an object. The deeper the missile penetrated, the nastier the wound became; and if the bullet passed through the body, it tore everything around it on the way out.

In those cases where the rifle ball pierced through and out of the body or a limb, the surgeon would clean out the entrance and exit. He might pack the injured area with rags soaked in salt water. Otherwise, he left the open and filthy wound to heal itself.

When the bullet had fractured a joint or broken a bone in the arm or leg, the only treatment was amputation—cutting off the limb. Amputation was the most common operation at a field hospital. Liquid anesthetics such as chloroform and ether were known at the time, but they were in short supply. If whiskey was available, it was used as a painkiller.

Several hundred soldiers who lost a limb to the surgeon's knife did so without benefit of any kind of medicine to ease the pain. That is why surgeons performing amputations worked as fast as they could. The truly good Civil War surgeon could cut through muscle, saw through bone, and have the mangled limb out of the way in less than five minutes.

Infection, especially dreaded and incurable gangrene, followed most amputations. Then came long days and nights of intense pain until death finally ended the suffering.

Thousands of wounded soldiers died from lack of attention. In October 1861, several hundred sick Confederate soldiers gathered at the railroad station at Manassas Junction in Virginia. Rain was falling, but no provisions had been made for receiving the men. They stood in the cold downpour for several hours. None of them had raincoats; only a few owned a blanket.

Finally the train arrived. The men climbed painfully into dirty boxcars and, without food, water, or care of any kind, endured the hundred-mile

Cutting off damaged limbs was the most common operation performed on Civil War soldiers, as these five Union veterans could attest. (National Library of Medicine)

ride to Richmond. At the capital there was no one to meet them. Those soldiers who were still alive lay helplessly at the depot or stumbled down the streets in search of aid.

Scenes after a battle were equally horrible.

In 1863, after the battle of Gettysburg, a medical inspector on the Union side wrote that the week following the battle was "the occasion of the greatest amount of human suffering known to this nation since its birth." Some 22,000 wounded soldiers were packed into a town of 2,000 citizens. The number of men waiting for medical attention grew so large that the surgeons grimly divided them into two groups: those who were likely to die and those who had a chance of being saved.

Stretcher-bearers took hundreds of men in the first group into woods nearby and laid them in rows. There they tossed and turned and screamed until death came. The second group remained at the field hospitals and continued the painful wait for treatment.

Lee's army, meanwhile, had started back to Virginia. General John Imboden was in charge of the ambulance wagons during the slow retreat from Gettysburg. The Virginia officer never forgot what he saw on that march. Imboden stated: "For four hours I hurried forward on my way to the front, and in all that time I was never out of hearing of the groans and cries of the wounded and dying. Scarcely one in a hundred had received adequate surgical aid. . . . Many of the wounded in the wagons had been without food for thirty-six hours. Their torn and bloody clothing, matted and hardened, was rasping the tender, inflamed, and still oozing wounds. Very few of the wagons had even a layer of straw in them, and all were without springs. The road was rough and rocky. . . . From nearly every wagon . . . came such cries and shrieks as these:

" 'O God! Why can't I die?'

" 'My God! Will no one have mercy and kill me?'

" 'Stop! Oh! for God's sake, stop just for one minute. Take me out and leave me to die on the roadside!'

" 'I am dying! I am dying! My poor wife, my dear children, what will become of you?'

"No help could be rendered to any of the sufferers," said Imboden. "No heed could be given to any of their appeals. . . . There was no time even to fill a canteen with water for a dying man. . . . During this one night I realized more of the horrors of war than I had in all the two preceding years."

U.S. hospital ship. (Private collection)

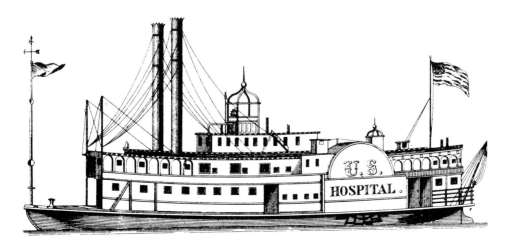

14

1864: Tightening the Noose

"GRANT IS MY MAN," Lincoln announced after the Union victory at Vicksburg, "and I am his the rest of the war." In March 1864, Lincoln summoned Grant to Washington and made him general in chief of all Union armies. The promotion was well deserved, and it brought a dramatic shift in Northern strategy.

Too often in the first part of the war, Union generals had fought as if they were in a chess game where one moves his pieces and maneuvers into position to capture the king—the enemy's capital—and end the game. Grant did not think of war that way. His idea was to play not chess but checkers: to concentrate his forces, attack each of the enemy's pieces, and keep driving ahead until he had swept the board clean of all resistance. The enemy's armies and resources, not just its capital, would all be major targets.

Such activity is known as total war. It was this strategy that destroyed the Confederacy and ended the Civil War.

Grant announced that he would not command the Federal armies from a desk in Washington. Rather, he would direct overall operations from the field while traveling with the Army of the Potomac. Lee's Confederates in the East would occupy Grant's attention. To command the Federal forces in the West, Grant chose his friend and proven leader, General William T. Sherman.

The 1864 battle plan that Grant developed in Virginia was sweeping but simple. Lee might be able to defend some points, but his limited forces could not defend all points. Grant therefore determined to strike everywhere.

He ordered four different Federal columns to advance into Virginia at the same time. Grant, with General Meade's Army of the Potomac, would seek out and attack Lee again and again. General Philip Sheridan's Federal cavalry would circle around Lee's flank and make a raid on Richmond. The new Army of the James, with politician-turned-general Benjamin Franklin Butler at its head, would advance along the river for which it was named and attack Richmond from the east while Grant and Lee were locked in combat. General Franz Sigel and a fourth column of Federals would push into the Shenandoah Valley, destroy food sources, and come at Lee from the west for the "final kill."

Northern officials confidently thought that this all-engaging offensive would take about two months to succeed. In reality, it led to eleven months of almost continuous fighting. The first stages of Grant's master plan were unexpected failures and cost the lives of an incredible number of men.

On May 4, the Army of the Potomac, 115,000 strong, crossed the Rapidan River in Virginia. Grant's plan was to sneak through the same thickly wooded Wilderness region where Hooker had met defeat a year earlier. He would then advance into the open country well beyond Lee's flank. However, Lee's 64,000 soldiers were waiting for the Federals in the darkness of the Wilderness. Grant's army was strung out along a single-lane country road on May 5 when thousands of Johnny Rebs attacked from the west along two other, parallel roads.

The battle of the Wilderness was an infantryman's contest because there were few clearings that artillery could use. Three country roads inside dense woods were the scenes of vicious fighting. For two long days, the troops of Grant and Lee blindly attacked back and forth through woods and underbrush. Soldiers fired at smoke and sound, for no one could see the enemy. Each came close to breaking the other's line.

Both sides were exhausted when the Wilderness fighting ended. It had been a battle with a new level of horror. Musket fire set a portion of the dry woods ablaze. Throughout the struggle, soldiers too badly wounded to gain safety were burned to death by the flames.

Union casualties at the Wilderness were 2,200 killed and 15,000 wounded. Lee's losses were about 11,000—roughly one of every five Confederates he had. Yet Grant had been stopped. The Army of the Potomac had suffered another defeat.

The Federals did not retreat as they had done in 1862 and 1863.

Rifle fire set the woods ablaze during the battle of the Wilderness. Here Union soldiers are carrying an injured man to safety in a makeshift sling while other wounded soldiers, unable to move, beg for help. (Harper's Weekly)

Grant had no intention of letting up or giving up. He knew that he had more troops and more supplies than Lee did, as well as the full confidence of Lincoln. So the Union commander led his army not north but southeast. His aim was to go around Lee's right flank and place the Federals between Lee and Richmond.

Lee rapidly marched his tired soldiers to meet the new threat. At Spotsylvania, a few miles from the Wilderness, the two armies again met in battle. This campaign lasted two weeks. The worst fighting occurred on May 12 when thousands of Federals drove against a V-shaped point in the Confederate line. The point was first called the Salient. After the battle, it was known as Bloody Angle.

For twenty hours—in rain, mud, and darkness—soldiers of North and South fought an almost inhuman battle for control of a single line of earthworks. Close to 15,000 men fell, most of them along only 400 yards of Confederate line. Lee barely managed to hold his position.

In all, the struggle for Spotsylvania cost Grant another 11,000 troops. Lee's casualties were fewer than a third of that number, about 4,000. Grant could draw on the vast manpower of the North to fill the gaps in his ranks. Lee had no reservoir from which he could obtain new soldiers. One dirty and weary Johnny Reb summed up the situation by commenting: "What's the use of killing those fellows? Kill one and half a dozen take his place."

Meanwhile, Sheridan's blueclad horsemen were accomplishing a good deal on their Richmond raid. The 10,000 Federal troopers destroyed miles of railroad and badly frightened the citizens of the capital. In a May 11 cavalry fight on the outskirts of Richmond, Federals mortally wounded Jeb Stuart, Lee's cavalry chief. Sheridan knew that he could not remain so far inside enemy territory. He and his cavalry galloped to safety inside the Army of the James and later rejoined Grant's army.

Spotsylvania, one of the most intense battles of the entire war. (Battles and Leaders of the Civil War)

Following Spotsylvania, Grant continued moving to the southeast in still another effort to turn Lee's right and get behind his lines. Three more days of occasional fighting exploded along the North Anna River. After that the two armies seemed locked in a struggle to the death as they moved together closer to Richmond. On June 2, at a crossroads known as Cold Harbor, Lee's forces were again squarely across Grant's front. The Union general lost his patience. He ordered a frontal assault against Lee to be made the next morning.

Many of the Billy Yanks, wise to the ways of war by now, knew that this attack had little chance of success. Just before going into battle, they wrote their names and units on pieces of paper and pinned them to their shirts so that their dead bodies could be identified.

The battle of Cold Harbor was indeed a massacre. On June 3, in about two hours of fighting, 7,000 Federals were killed or crippled. Grant refused to ask for a truce to bury his dead and collect his wounded. Scores of fallen Billy Yanks died in agony over the next three days.

By then, cries of outrage were coming from all over the North. In a month of fighting, Grant had lost 55,000 men—and he was no closer to Richmond than McClellan had been two years earlier. Grant was unmoved by all the criticism. "I propose to fight it out on this line if it takes all summer," he vowed.

It would take even longer than that because the other Federal thrusts in Virginia had been even less successful.

General Butler's 30,000 Federals in the Army of the James had moved by boat toward Richmond while Grant struggled in the Wilderness. Butler landed his forces at City Point, midway between Richmond and Petersburg. The Federal commander then seemed to lose his confidence. He made a halfhearted strike at Richmond and then paused to consider his situation.

A Confederate force under General P.G.T. Beauregard suddenly appeared from Petersburg. Butler drew back his army to a neck of land between the James and Appomattox rivers. Beauregard quickly threw a line of earthworks across the opening through which Butler had passed. The Army of the James, an angry Grant stated, was "as completely shut off from further operations against Richmond as if it had been in a bottle strongly corked."

Federals in the Shenandoah Valley stumbled into an even worse disaster. Sigel and his 8,000 soldiers had advanced southward as far as the village of New Market. There, on May 15, they came under attack from a hodgepodge Confederate force of 5,000 men. Included in this "army" were 263 teenage cadets from the Virginia Military Institute at Lexington.

The Confederates delivered a sharp attack in steady rain. They overran Sigel's position and sent the Federals fleeing down the valley. Among the Southern casualties were ten VMI cadets killed and forty-seven wounded.

General David Hunter replaced the bumbling Sigel. A month later, Hunter's army burned its way through the Shenandoah as far as Lexington. The Federals turned east, only to be stopped at Lynchburg and sent in retreat into the mountains west of the valley.

After Cold Harbor, it was obvious to Grant that he could not go through or around Lee's army and get to Richmond. Twenty miles south of the rebel capital lay Petersburg. It was the junction for most of the railroads coming out of the South. Capturing it would make Richmond indefensible. So Grant tried one more "sidling" movement to the southeast.

In mid-June, Grant disappeared from Lee's front, took his army across the James River, and moved rapidly in his first campaign for Petersburg. Attacks on that city by the lead units of the Federal army were weak and uncoordinated, despite the fact that Union soldiers outnumbered Confederates by five to one. As the full Northern army arrived in front of Petersburg, so did the Southern forces from north of the James. Lee and Grant faced each other again.

The Federal commander had lost 64,000 men since the campaign began in May. Now he had advanced as far as he could. Grant then determined to do in Virginia what he had done so well at Vicksburg, Mississippi. He would spread out his army and use siege warfare to wear out his enemy, who now had to defend both Richmond and Petersburg.

Grant knew that time was on his side. The Confederates could not hold out forever. Half of Lee's army had fallen in battle from the Wilderness to Petersburg. Grant was also aware of an equally important fact. Keeping Lee penned in the miles of trenches from east of Richmond to south of Petersburg would stop the swift movements and skillful strikes that had made him such a worthy opponent.

Sadly, Lee knew this too. When the campaign had first begun, Lee commented of his forces: "This army cannot stand a siege. We must end this business on the battlefield, not in a fortified place."

Shovels replaced muskets as thousands of Billy Yanks constructed miles of connecting earthworks around Petersburg and extending toward Richmond. Supplies and reinforcements poured into the Union lines from Grant's river base at City Point. The longest siege in American history was underway.

That autumn, Grant moved to prevent Lee from getting food from the Shenandoah Valley. He dispatched one of his favorite generals, Sheridan, and a large army to finish what Sigel and Hunter had started. Grant's instructions to Sheridan were brutal but necessary: "If the war is to last another year," Grant said, "we want the Shenandoah Valley to remain a barren waste."

Sheridan obeyed his orders to the fullest. Federals smashed into General Jubal Early's outmanned Confederates first at Opequon Creek, then at Fisher's Hill, and finally at Cedar Creek. Then Sheridan captured or destroyed livestock, fields, storehouses, farm buildings, and orchards so completely that the rich Shenandoah Valley turned into a vast wasteland.

Meanwhile, in the West, General William T. Sherman had begun what would become one of the most famous offensives of the entire war. It was

Grant used huge mortars like this one to bombard Lee's lines at Petersburg, Virginia. These guns could hurl a 200-pound missile larger than a basketball a distance of two and a half miles. (Library of Congress)

a campaign that would tear the Confederacy apart and break the will of the Southern people.

"Uncle Billy" Sherman was a professional soldier with modern ideas. In 1864, he sternly observed: "We cannot change the hearts of those people of the South, but we can make war so terrible and make them so sick of it that generations would pass away before they would again appeal to it." Sherman accomplished that with the forces he unleashed that spring.

On May 7, Sherman left Chattanooga, Tennessee, on his campaign. His objective was Atlanta, Georgia: rail junction, manufacturing center, and the heart of what was left of the Deep South. To get there, Sherman planned to march along the vital Western & Atlantic Railroad. He had a veteran army of over 100,000 men.

Opposed to him were 65,000 equally tested Confederates. They were under General Joseph E. Johnston, who had replaced Bragg after the mismanaged battles of Lookout Mountain and Missionary Ridge. Johnston knew what Sherman planned to do. How to stop him was another matter.

Sherman's march to Atlanta took four months. Johnston could not risk a great battle in the hundred miles of open and undefended country between Chattanooga and Atlanta. He had to be content with hit-and-run combat: fight awhile here, fall back to there, fight awhile there, fall back to another good position, but always protect Atlanta in the process.

During May and June, the two armies clashed eight times in northwest Georgia. At Kennesaw Mountain, the site of one of those battles, Sherman delivered an unwise series of frontal assaults just as Grant had done at Cold Harbor, Virginia. The repulse cost Sherman 3,000 casualties to Johnston's 600 losses.

Still, by mid-July, Sherman had fought his way to the outskirts of Atlanta. Johnston's troops had taken refuge in the earthworks surrounding the city. President Davis led the chorus of Southern complaints that Johnston had allowed Sherman to get within sight of Atlanta. On July 17, the president fired Johnston and assigned General John B. Hood to take charge of the Army of Tennessee.

Hood had lost the use of an arm at Gettysburg and one of his legs at Chickamauga. He was young and brave—too much so, perhaps. Barely two days after taking command, Hood attacked part of Sherman's army at Peachtree Creek. Superior Federal numbers beat back the assaults. Undaunted, Hood attacked another part of Sherman's line two days later.

This all-afternoon battle of Atlanta brought heavy losses on both sides. By nightfall, Hood was back inside his defenses and the Federal lines were intact.

Sherman then followed Grant's favorite tactic and began a siege. Slowly the huge Federal army extended its position west and south around Atlanta. On July 28, Hood tried to stop the stranglehold with an assault at Ezra Church. It was as bloody a failure as the two other battles at Atlanta had been. Sherman pressed harder to tighten his hold on Atlanta.

On the last day of August, with Sherman's men about to cut the last rail line from Atlanta, the Confederates made a desperate attack at Jonesboro. It too was a failure. This setback doomed Atlanta.

Hood abandoned the city and headed south. On September 2, with bands playing, Sherman's army marched through the rubble of the once-proud city. "Atlanta is ours, and fairly won," Sherman stated in a wire to the War Department. When news of Atlanta's fall reached Richmond, the wife of a Confederate official wrote sadly: "We are going to be wiped off the earth."

The capture of Atlanta was the Union's most outstanding military success that year, and Sherman's victory ensured Lincoln's reelection in November. The Northern people were now more determined than ever to fight—and to win—the war.

Sherman converted Atlanta into a military fortress and kept it that way for two months. He ordered all civilians from the city. As residents left in a steady stream, Federal supplies entered Atlanta on wagons and rail cars. Hood and his battered 40,000 Confederates swung around Atlanta to the west. They marched northwest toward Tennessee with the hope of forcing Sherman's army out of the city.

It did not work. Sherman sent a third of his forces back to Tennessee to make sure that enough Federals would be on hand to confront Hood's Confederates. Then Sherman started on his most famous drive. On November 15, he set fire to everything of military value inside Atlanta. As he watched from a hilltop, flames spread quickly and consumed a third of the city. Sherman turned east with 60,000 troops and started across Georgia on a 285-mile march to Savannah, near the Atlantic Ocean.

Sherman's men met little resistance. How much unnecessary damage they did remains one of the Civil War's leading controversies. Invading soldiers tend to plunder and destroy whatever they encounter. Sherman did not give orders for such acts. Nor did he try to stop them. The "March

The ruins of the railroad depot in Atlanta, Georgia, after Sherman burned and then abandoned the city. (National Archives)

to the Sea" brought more destruction to farms and communities than any other campaign of the Civil War. Sherman would later estimate the damage he caused at one hundred million dollars.

On December 22, five weeks after leaving Atlanta, Sherman obtained his goal. He sent a telegram to Lincoln and presented Savannah, Georgia, to the president as a Christmas gift. The Union army had reached the Atlantic coast and cut the South in two.

What happened to the Confederacy's second-largest army late that year was another cause for Southern despair. As Sherman marched east toward Savannah, Hood's mostly barefooted Southerners limped north into Tennessee. On November 30, the Army of Tennessee met Federal forces just south of Nashville at Franklin. Once again Hood carelessly ordered a frontal assault against strong entrenchments.

With no artillery support, Johnny Rebs swept across a mile of open

Midway through the war, soldiers began fighting from behind earthworks, but these defenses did not always provide protection. (Battles and Leaders of the Civil War)

country against well-protected Federals. Waiting Billy Yanks cheered the heroism of their enemy at first. Then they opened fire. In less than an hour, 6,300 Confederates lay dead or wounded. Six Confederate generals were killed. In all, twelve generals and fifty-four regimental colonels in Hood's army were lost in the battle.

The Federals fell back to their main lines at Nashville. The city had been strongly fortified during its three years of Union occupation, and General George Henry Thomas's army outnumbered Hood almost two to one. Hood should have retreated. Instead, he advanced on Nashville with barely a hope of winning some kind of victory. Bitingly cold weather and heavy Federal numbers forced Hood to a halt in front of the city.

Thomas calmly waited for an ice storm to pass and melt away. Then, on December 15, the Union commander sent waves of Federals charging against Hood's left flank. Billy Yanks soon poured over the Confederate lines. Hood fell back, only to be assailed again the next day. Darkness on the sixteenth found the beaten Southerners in flight—men, horses, cannon, and wagons all hurrying southward through rain in total defeat. The mighty Army of Tennessee had lost 35,000 of 50,000 soldiers in five months. All that was left of the Confederate army, Thomas said with a mixture of pride and sadness, was a "ragged, bloody" fragment, "without food and without hope."

Horrors of Prison Life

The Civil War era was the only time America has ever faced the problem of large numbers of enemy prisoners. Nearly 409,000 soldiers were captured—four or five times more than in all of our other wars combined. Neither the Union nor the Confederacy knew what to do with these men, and more than 56,000 of them died while in the hands of the enemy.

The story of Civil War prisons is the ugliest, and in many ways the saddest, part of the war. It is a story of neglect and suffering. North and South were equally guilty of overcrowding, mismanagement, and providing inadequate facilities. Many of the twenty to twenty-five major prisons were on swamp-

In the foreground of this rare photograph of Andersonville Prison is the prisoners' latrine, or open toilet. (Library of Congress)

land or in open country with no trees to provide shelter or firewood. From every compound came the same sickening reports of filth, vermin, disease, poor food, lack of sanitation, brutal guards, and insufficient medical care. These in turn produced widespread sickness, mental depression, and— for thousands of prisoners —slow death.

Prison routine was drab and monotonous. The men arose at dawn, answered roll call, and received something to eat. For the rest of the day they did nothing. Prisoners received a second meal in late afternoon. Another roll call was taken at sundown. The next day was the same, as was each day thereafter.

Fleas and lice were a major part of every prison population. A New York soldier described the vermin in his prison: "The beasts crawled over the ground from body to body, and their attacks seemed to become more aggravating as the men became more [frail]."

Cruel guards were also a common presence. Of a trio of prison officials at Fort Del-

aware, Delaware, a Tennessee soldier wrote bitterly: "I Don't Think Thar is any Place in Hell Hot Anuf for Thos 3 men."

None of the prisons had sufficient medical supplies, and surgeons were not always the most competent or most caring. Since many of the soldiers had fallen into enemy hands because they were too sick or wounded to escape, and since prison life offered nothing to make a man well, death was a daily event in every Civil War compound.

Many of the more able-bodied soldiers tried to escape. Only a few were successful in making their way back to friendly lines. The great majority of prisoners, a captured Billy Yank observed, "sit moping for hours with a look of utter dejection, their elbow upon their knee, and their chin resting upon their hand, their eyes having a vacant, far-away look."

Andersonville, a prison camp for Federals in Georgia, was the largest of the Civil War compounds. It consisted of twenty-six acres of treeless ground, with no shelter except what the prisoners themselves were able to make. Of the 52,300 Federals imprisoned at Andersonville during its one-year history, more than 13,200 died. At a prison camp for captured Confederates at Elmira, New York, a quarter of the inmates perished in a twelve-month period.

The only monuments to the agony and death in Civil War prisons are soldier cemeteries at the sites where many of the compounds were located.

Twelve-man Sibley tent; named for its inventor. (Private collection)

15

Life on the Homefront

WOMEN OF THE 1860s proved extremely valuable in several areas previously dominated by men. The first was in teaching school. As men left the schoolhouse for the army in increasing numbers, more need arose for teachers. Women sprang forward to help. The word *schoolmistress* became more familiar than *schoolmaster*.

Both North and South employed hundreds of women as clerks, secretaries, and factory workers. More than 200 women in Columbia, South Carolina, worked in the Confederate Treasury Note Bureau. In one Massachusetts clothing factory, 500 seamstresses produced 1,000 uniform shirts per day.

Many young women accepted dangerous positions in ordnance (weapons) plants. They made bullets and worked with explosive materials. Some of them lost their lives at these tasks. In March 1863, an explosion at a Confederate ordnance laboratory killed fifty women and their child-helpers.

Another great contribution by women was made in the field of nursing. Before 1861, a respectable woman did not visit a hospital with all of its suffering, blood, odors, and filth. Male nurses—such as the poet Walt Whitman—tended to the first waves of sick and wounded in the Civil War. As the number of injured soldiers multiplied with each passing month, the cry for more nurses grew louder.

Women answered the call. Judith McGuire of Virginia worked in a Confederate government department by day and served as a volunteer nurse in Richmond hospitals at night. What one woman learned, she taught to

ABOVE: *Women making bullets in a Northern weapons plant. (Harper's Weekly)*
BELOW: *Hundreds of women worked as nurses during the Civil War, assisting in operations, changing bandages, and, as shown here, reading to wounded soldiers. (Harper's Weekly)*

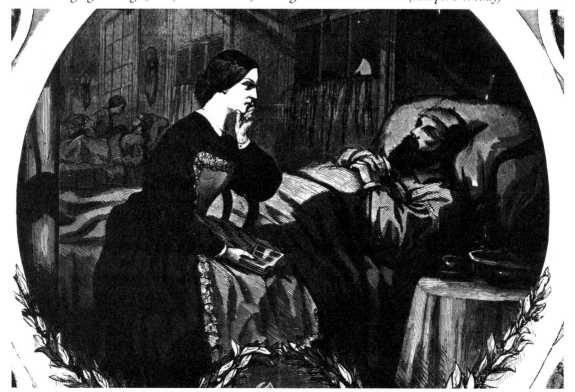

another. The work was hard and dangerous. Author Louisa May Alcott had been a nurse for only a month in Northern hospitals when she became ill with typhoid fever. Doctors gave her too much of the wrong kind of medicine. As a result, Miss Alcott lost several teeth and much of her hair, and suffered permanent damage to her nervous system.

The first hours of duty for any volunteer nurse were the worst. Belle Reynolds of Illinois offered to assist one surgeon after the battle of Shiloh. She almost fainted at the sight she beheld. This young woman never forgot the surgeon's "glittering knife and saw," and how a "severed limb, white as snow and spattered with blood, would fall upon the floor."

In Richmond, Sally Tompkins converted an old home into a hospital. She proved to be such a devoted nurse that President Davis appointed her a captain of cavalry to give her infirmary recognition as an army hospital. Miss Tompkins was the only woman ever to hold an official military status in the Confederate armies. During the Civil War, her hospital alone housed 1,300 sick and wounded soldiers.

One of the more colorful of Civil War nurses was blunt but warmhearted Mary Ann Bickerdyke. When she went to work in a Federal military hospital, Mrs. Bickerdyke made her position plain. "Them generals and all ain't going to stop me," she declared. "This is the Lord's work."

Everyone called her "Mother Bickerdyke" because she treated sick soldiers as though they were her sons. Even stern General Sherman paused to express thanks for her work. A colonel's wife once complained to Sherman: Mrs. Bickerdyke, overburdened by patients, had refused to nurse the woman's ill son. The general snapped back: "You've picked on the one person around here who outranks me. If you want to lodge a complaint against her, you'll have to take it to President Lincoln!"

Soldiers blue and gray crippled each other in battle, but behind the lines the nurses treated friend and foe alike. Eliza Harris served aboard a Federal hospital ship. She once commented: "I was obliged to wash all my skirts, as they were saturated with the mingled blood of the Union and Confederate soldiers."

Equally touching is the statement of Fannie Beers, a volunteer nurse working in Atlanta: "My hands and dress and feet were bloody, and I felt sick with horror. I had not been five minutes in the ward, where lay the most dangerously wounded Federals, when all animosity vanished and my woman's heart melted."

Life for Southern women during the Civil War was especially severe. Even when Confederate money was available (which was rare), the paper dollars had less and less value while prices rose steadily higher. This inflation prevented people from buying the necessities of life. In 1864, a Virginia housewife complained that she took her money to the market in a shopping bag and brought home her purchases in a pocketbook.

At a time when a female employee in Richmond made seven dollars a day, a pound of butter cost four dollars, a dozen eggs were twenty dollars, and a barrel of corn—when one could be found—was at least fifty dollars.

Half of the Southern white families belonged to the lower economic classes. Poverty in the South became more intense as the war years passed. A larger proportion of men from the South went into the armies. No government relief agencies, as existed in the North, were available in the Confederacy to help homefolk in distress.

Advancing Union armies were always a danger for Southern civilians; and when those forces were under generals Pope, Hunter, Sheridan, and Sherman, Southern civilians in their path were reduced to destitution.

The Union naval blockade prevented badly needed goods, especially medicines, from entering the Confederacy. Lack of supplies, worthless money, dangerous health situations, and attacks from lawless groups roaming the countryside brought misery to the Confederate homefront.

Most Confederate wives had children equal in number to the years they had been married. What meager wages the soldiers sent home were likely to be lost in the mail. Since three out of four Southern families did not own slaves, the women left behind on the farms had to do everything.

They performed their household duties, planted the crops, plowed the fields, and brought in the harvest. They killed the hogs, cured the meat, cut the firewood, and attended to all the other farm chores. Seizure of horses, mules, and cattle by government authorities crippled both farm production and food supply. As goods disappeared in the wartime South, wives and mothers had to make their own soap, candles, leather, cloth, and coloring dyes.

When their children became ill, the women had to care for them as best they could. Home remedies were the only available medicines. They usually did not work. Watching helplessly as a child slowly died was terrible enough; the mother had to dig the grave, wrap the child and bury it, then endure a broken heart without the support of her husband far away.

Such was the case with a Mississippi mother who wrote to her husband in Lee's army: "Twenty grains of quinine would have saved our two children. They were too nauseated to drink the bitter willow tea and they are now at rest, and I have no one to work for but you. I am not dismayed. I think day and night of your sorrow. I [at least] have their little graves near me."

The shortage of food was a constant hardship for Confederate women. They fell back to using crude substitutes for basic foodstuffs. In place of sugar, Southern women had to use thinned molasses, honey, and watermelon juice. Strawberry or blackberry leaves took the place of tea. Crushed corn or dried sweet potato was a poor substitute for coffee. To get salt, which was necessary both for good health and for curing meat, women would strain the dirt from smokehouse floors where meat had been hung to age.

Firewood and axes were not always available. Women often had to use pine needles, leaves, and rotten wood in their stoves. During the win-

In this June 1862 cartoon from Harper's Weekly, an officer in Union-held Memphis, Tennessee, warns a restaurant owner about the dangers of advertising. (The Granger Collection)

A DANGEROUS NOVELTY IN MEMPHIS.

OFFICER OF THE PROVOST GUARD. "Hi! look here, you Eating-House Keeper. Take that Mutton Chop out of your Window, or we shall have a riot, presently!"

ter, many Southern families lived only in one room because there was not enough firewood to heat the entire home.

Crude candles were made by weaving a few strands of thread together and dipping them into melted beeswax. Carpets were taken from the floor and used as blankets. Dresses were patchwork affairs, with good pieces from several ragged garments sewn together. If some coloring was desired, certain plants could be boiled to produce different dyes. Pine roots, for example, gave a deep red color, a myrtle bush yielded a shade of gray, and mashed acorns and walnuts produced a light tan dye known as butternut.

Shoes were the hardest item to obtain. In warm weather, poor people had always gone barefoot to save what shoes they had. Many women made shoes with wooden boards for soles and leather straps for tops. One Confederate wife produced footwear with soles made of horseshoes and pieces of string as straps.

Many women could not write, nor could their husbands or sons in the army read. Those civilians capable of sending letters sometimes found the task even more difficult because of the scarcity of writing materials. Pens and pencils were in short supply. Paper was never plentiful. Southern women often used wallpaper and old newspapers for stationery.

When they had writing paper, some women used it to the fullest. They would write a page, turn it upside down and write between the lines, then turn the page sideways and write some more. This enabled the correspondent to put seven or eight pages on the front and back of a single sheet.

Loneliness was a common emotion among Civil War women. A letter here and there, a short furlough (leave from military duty), were the only means of contact between the man in the army and his family back home. This meant that mothers and wives could go for weeks—even months—without knowing whether their sons or husbands were still alive.

Some of the hardest blows of the Civil War fell upon women. In November 1862, Sarah Mills of Des Moines, Iowa, received a short note that her husband, father, and brother had all been slain at the battle of Corinth, Mississippi. Her tragedy seems mild when compared to that of Polly Ray, a widow in Cumberland County, North Carolina. She lost all seven of her sons in the war.

Many women bore hardships like these with heroic determination. A Florida girl wrote in 1863: "The armies must be supplied even if the home-folks starve. They must not have our burdens to bear in addition to their own." A year earlier, a North Carolina wife wrote her husband: "I would not have you leave your country's service as long as she needs you and you can serve. Do your duty to God and man . . . and you will have a clear conscience and your children the heritage of a good name."

Another farmer's wife sought to cheer up her soldier-husband with a homemade poem:

> Leave the corn upon the stalks, John,
> Potatoes on the hill,
> And the pumpkin on the vine, John,
> I'll gather them with a will.
> Then take your gun and go, John,
> Take your gun and go.
> Ruth can drive the oxen, John,
> And *I* can use the hoe.

This Southern wife was not among the lucky ones whose husbands returned home. Her photograph was found beside a dead Confederate soldier at Chancellorsville. (Museum of the Confederacy)

Late in the war, a North Carolina soldier went on trial for desertion. The man was guilty; he had fled the army. What saved him from a firing squad was a letter found in his pocket. It was from his wife. His life was spared because of what the letter said:

My dear Edward—I have always been proud of you, and since your connection with the Confederate army, I have been prouder of you than ever before. I would not have you do anything wrong for the world, but before God, Edward, unless you come home we must die. Last night I was aroused by little Eddie crying. I called out and said, "What is the matter, Eddie?" and he said, "O mamma! I am so hungry" And Lucy, Edward, your darling Lucy; she never complains, but she is getting thinner and thinner every day. And before God, Edward, unless you come home we must die. Your Mary.

No one can blame this hard-pressed wife for the despair that she felt. Day by day, with the men away in the army, Southern women had to stay alive in a torn and wrecked country. Their children had to be fed and clothed, yet there was little food and even less clothing. Where their loved ones were—and what condition they were in—led to constant worry and sleepless nights. Yet through the long months of weariness, separation, danger, and need, overwhelming numbers of Southern women remained loyal and brave citizens of their country.

Just as the women of the South stood firm in the war, so did most of them accept the sadness of defeat. The lucky ones took comfort that their menfolk came home. "Your General lives, My Colonel lives," a South Carolina wife told a friend in 1865. "What words can express our gratitude." When all the men in her family returned safely from the war, a North Carolina lady cried: "The sense of duty done, and the knowledge of God's providence overriding all things filled us with joy and peace, and we exclaimed: 'The Lord is good.'"

16

1865: The Birth of a Nation

THE END WAS COMING, and there was nothing the South could do about it. Inside the battered Confederacy, food was scarce, clothing was in short supply, and medicines did not exist. Money for buying goods was no longer worth even the paper and ink required to print it. Natural resources had been used up. With one or two exceptions, the South's few factories were silent. The people of the Confederacy, discouraged and in need, were rapidly losing the will to continue the war.

Throughout the war years, Federal warships had tightened the blockade of the Southern coast. By 1865, all of the Confederate ports had been sealed except Charleston, South Carolina, and Wilmington, North Carolina. The Southern nation now consisted only of Virginia and the Carolinas. They were on the verge of collapsing from Federal military pressure.

In Virginia, Grant had pinned down the main Confederate army in a line extending twenty-five miles from Richmond to Petersburg. Lee's forces, unable to move, were slowly dying in the trenches. All Lee could do was wait helplessly for Grant to attack. Grant would surely do this as soon as spring came and the snow and mud of winter disappeared.

On February 1, 1865, Sherman's battle-hardened troops began the grand and final drive against the Confederacy. The Federal general and his 60,000 soldiers cut loose from Savannah just as they had done at Atlanta. Now they would smash to the north, not to the east. Sherman would destroy everything in his path as he headed through the Carolinas to join Grant's army.

It was one of the most remarkable advances of the war. Sherman's

Federals marched nearly 450 miles through enemy territory in forty-five days. It rained for twenty-eight of those days.

Scattered Confederate units desperately tried to block Sherman's advance. General William Joseph Hardee had several thousand troops in South Carolina, but too many of them were home guard units with no battle experience. A veteran cavalry leader, General Wade Hampton, put together all the horse soldiers he could muster. From Tennessee, about 18,000 more Confederates marched painfully across the scarred lands of the South to lend help. They were all that was left of the Army of Tennessee.

Following the battle of Nashville the previous December, Hood had asked to be relieved of army command. Robert E. Lee, appointed in late January 1865 as the first general in chief of all Confederate forces, soon named the still-popular "Uncle Joe" Johnston to lead the Southern units trying to stop Sherman.

It took weeks for these Confederates to assemble. Sherman used that time to strike into South Carolina. Federal soldiers stepped up their looting and burning for good reasons, they asserted. South Carolina was the first Southern state to leave the Union; the bombardment of Fort Sumter in Charleston harbor had started the Civil War. "Here is where treason began," one of Sherman's privates wrote of South Carolina, "and by God, here is where it shall end!"

On February 17, Sherman's men marched into the state capital of Columbia. That night half of the city went up in flames. A combination of Federal military behavior and Southern civil disorder probably accounted for the burning of Columbia. The next day the other great city in the Palmetto State fell to Union forces. Charleston, cut off from the rest of South Carolina by Sherman's advance, was helpless. Confederates retreated from the port. The "Queen City of the South" now lay abandoned and useless.

Sherman's army continued its destructive march northward with hardly a pause. When other Union troops captured Wilmington, North Carolina, on February 22, the Confederacy lost its last major seaport. More importantly for Sherman, Federals quickly converted Wilmington into their own supply base. On March 11, Sherman occupied Fayetteville, North

A huge stockpile of supplies for Grant's army during the siege of Petersburg. This picture was taken by Mathew Brady, best-known of a dozen photographers who made the Civil War the first photographed war in history. (The Bettmann Archive)

Carolina, at the headwaters of the Cape Fear River. There he met Union ships from Wilmington loaded with troops and supplies. Sherman burned the arsenal at Fayetteville. Then, with his army swelled to 86,000 well-rested and well-fed soldiers, Sherman resumed his advance toward Virginia.

Johnston and his Confederates were hopelessly outnumbered. However, the Southern general had to do something to try and stop Sherman. With the Federal army marching in two widely separated wings, Johnston decided to throw everything he had against the left half of Sherman's forces in North Carolina. He did that at Bentonville on March 19. Fighting lasted for most of three days. Sherman soon brought his two wings together and forced the Confederates from the field. In one of the many human tragedies of Bentonville, Confederate general Hardee's sixteen-year-old son was killed in the last Southern charge.

Sherman then moved to the railroad junction at Goldsboro and prepared to march on Raleigh. Johnston continued to fall back slowly through North Carolina.

In Virginia during those first months of 1865, Lee's position had become pitiful in every respect. Grant had used the long months of the siege of Richmond and Petersburg to make the most of his superior numbers. Week after week the Union commander slowly spread his lines to the west, forcing Lee to do the same. However, the Confederate general did not have enough men to keep his defenses both extended and strong. By springtime, the Confederate position at Petersburg resembled a rubber band stretched to its fullest.

Worse than that, the Confederate army barely managed to avoid starvation during the winter. A little meat and bread were all that Johnny Rebs could expect. Sickness, disease, and desertion cut deeply into Lee's ranks.

Bitterly cold weather also took a heavy toll among the half-naked men. The poet Sidney Lanier was one of those suffering Confederate soldiers. He recalled that his ragged coat "afforded no protection to anything but the insects congregated in the seams of the same." Lee's 55,000 men were surviving on little more than devotion to duty.

Across the few hundred yards separating the two opposing armies, Grant had 120,000 fully equipped Federals waiting for orders to advance. But the ever-bold Lee beat Grant to the punch. On March 25, Confederates attacked a sector of the Union lines at Fort Stedman.

With this move, Lee hoped to break through the Federal position and force Grant to release his bulldog hold on Petersburg. The Southern troops actually captured Fort Stedman and occupied a mile of Federal entrenchments. Soon, however, Grant's reserves poured into the area and sent the Confederates reeling back to their lines. Lee's last chance of ending the siege had failed and cost him 3,800 men.

It was now Grant's turn. With cool precision he struck hard. Grant sent Sheridan with 17,000 infantry and 12,000 cavalry to the extreme right flank of Lee's lines. On April 1, Sheridan assaulted the Confederate works at the road junction of Five Forks. Federals broke through the earthworks and captured 5,000 Confederates, about half the Confederates manning the line.

The next day, Grant quickly followed this success by launching huge attacks all along the Petersburg line. Lee's army had fought a heroic defense for nine months. Now the Union tide was too great. Federals overran the Southern lines at almost every point. Lee was barely able to escape Grant's clutches by retreating across the Appomattox River.

Lee's withdrawal forced the Confederate government to abandon Richmond. Chaos reigned as government officials, refugees, and local citizens fled the capital. Rioting began in the streets. When the Confederates burned the arsenals and warehouses to destroy the government stores, high winds and exploding shells sent fires whipping out of control through the downtown area.

On the morning of April 3, Union columns marched into the city, ending a siege that had lasted nearly ten months. Many townspeople and hundreds of now-liberated slaves greeted the Federals with relief. Richmond by then was as battered and blackened as the country whose symbol it had been.

When the Confederate army left Petersburg, Lee's first intention was to follow the Richmond & Danville Railroad southwest to Danville. There he hoped to meet Johnston's Confederates and, together, face the Union armies. That plan collapsed when Federal cavalry galloped far to the west and crossed the railroad, blocking Lee's advance.

Lee turned to the northwest in an effort to reach Lynchburg and make a stand. Grant, now sensing the end, gave Lee no relief. Federals constantly pressed on Lee's rear guard and flanks as weary, half-starved Confederates struggled along. On April 6, Grant fell upon the rear of Lee's army at Sayler's Creek. The Confederates fought like "a tiger at bay," Sheridan later

Once-beautiful downtown Richmond, Virginia, was a smoking ruin when Federal soldiers marched into the capital in April 1865. (Frank Leslie's Illustrated Newspaper, April 29, 1865)

reported. Yet line after line of Federals rolled over the Southern position. The fighting that day cost Lee some 7,000 casualties—about a fourth of his army. Among the five generals taken prisoner at Sayler's Creek was Custis Lee, the commander's son.

Three days later the end came for the Army of Northern Virginia. Lee's exhausted troops had limped as far as Appomattox Court House. There they found themselves surrounded by Grant's army.

Lee then had to make a difficult decision. He could order his soldiers to scatter, each man escaping the best way he could. Thereafter, from the hills and woods and byways, Confederates could fight a guerrilla war, with little bands causing damage wherever they could and keeping civil war raging for generations to come. Or Lee could surrender himself and his army, thus ending the war once and for all.

Guerrilla warfare would be the natural action to take because most civil wars become such a struggle. However, Lee would have none of that. Guerrilla warfare, he said, would never bring the South the one thing it had wanted from the beginning: the chance to live its own way in peace.

Grant's terms of surrender that Palm Sunday, April 9, 1865, were extremely generous. Confederate soldiers would be sent home on parole rather than put in prison. Those men who owned horses could keep them for use in plowing the fields for the year's crops. Grant also agreed to issue food at once to the hungry Southern troops. Lee accepted the terms with gratitude.

A senseless and tragic incident only a week later almost destroyed the chances of peace. On the evening of April 14, a fanatic named John Wilkes Booth shot the careworn Lincoln as the president was attending a play at Ford's Theater in Washington. This first assassination of an American president sent waves of anger through the North and waves of despair through a helpless South. Lincoln's death, however, would have consequences farther down the road in the postwar period known as Reconstruction.

The surrender of Lee's army signaled the end of the Confederacy. Other Southern forces soon laid down their weapons. In North Carolina, Johnston's army found itself still alone, facing Sherman, but with no place to go.

Sherman moved quickly to stop the fighting there. This Union gen-

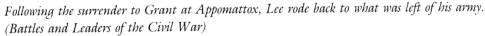

Following the surrender to Grant at Appomattox, Lee rode back to what was left of his army. (Battles and Leaders of the Civil War)

On April 14, 1865, John Wilkes Booth shot President Lincoln from behind as Lincoln watched a play at Ford's Theater. Federal troops pursued Booth to a farm in Virginia and killed him. (Harper's Weekly)

eral, so merciless in war, at first offered such lenient peace terms to Johnston that Federal authorities in Washington rejected them. Sherman then extended terms similar to those between Grant and Lee. On April 26, Johnston and the Army of Tennessee, the South's second-largest army, surrendered at Bennett Place, near Durham, North Carolina. Remaining Confederate troops in Louisiana and across the Mississippi stopped fighting during the next four weeks.

The long struggle had ended at last. Nearly eighty years earlier, the Founding Fathers had dreamed of a union of states. The first years of the republic had been a shaky experiment to see if a union would work. Now, from the smoke and fire of a great civil war, the United States became a reality.

Lincoln's hope for a peaceful reunion faded with his death, and the defeated South would undergo pain and humiliation during the military occupation by federal troops from 1867 to 1877. Yet the Civil War gave America a single definition, a single meaning, and a single purpose. We are one nation, one people. And the world has been much richer as a result.

17

Why the Civil War Still Lives

★ BITTER FIGHTING ENDED solemnly and honorably in 1865. The long-range effects of the Civil War have continued to this day. Several of those results had a dark side. Other legacies of the war were bright and truly nation-building.

The ten years following the Civil War were a sometimes sad period in American history. First, Abraham Lincoln's murder less than a week after Appomattox spread grief, anger, and uncertainty throughout much of the country. Lincoln was the first president slain in office. His sudden death shattered much of the happiness of peace.

Then Federal troops captured Jefferson Davis as the Confederate president fled southward in an effort to build a new government in Texas. Davis was placed in a military prison and held there without charge for two years. Such punishment made Davis a Southern hero. Until his death at the age of eighty-one, he was hailed by his people as a beloved symbol of what was called the "Lost Cause."

Meanwhile, tired and ragged Confederate soldiers had struggled home to a land where the hand of war had brought widespread destruction. One of every four white Southern males had died in the war. The task of rebuilding once-proud Dixieland would be long and difficult.

Fresh humiliation for the South came two years later. Radicals in Washington wanted to make sure that the Southern people would obey laws and no longer be a threat to national unity. In March 1867, the U.S. Congress passed the Military Reconstruction Act. Federal troops again marched into the South. They took control of Southern governments and

An 1867 woodcut engraving of Federal troops occupying New Orleans, Louisiana.
(The Bettmann Archive)

much of Southern life. For almost ten years, the people of the former Confederate states were the only Americans ever subjected to occupation and military law.

The indignity of Reconstruction, and the political corruption that took place throughout much of that period, left a bitterness in Southern hearts far deeper than that of losing the Civil War.

For most of the three and a half million former slaves, the postwar years were full of empty dreams and broken hopes. Lincoln's 1863 Emancipation Proclamation had promised freedom to Southern slaves. As one event after another showed, however, the victorious North proved no more willing to accept blacks as equals than was the defeated South.

It is true that constitutional changes on behalf of American blacks came about less than a decade after the Civil War. The Thirteenth Amendment of 1865 made the Emancipation Proclamation law by prohibiting slavery in the United States. Passage of the Fourteenth Amendment in 1868 promised equality to all citizens. The right to vote for every American male citizen, regardless of color, became law with the Fifteenth Amendment of 1870.

Passing these measures was a giant step forward. Making those laws work was a vastly different matter. Freed slaves who migrated to all parts

Cartoonist Thomas Nast made this drawing to show the corruption and chaos that often reigned in Southern state legislatures during Reconstruction. In the background is the figure of Peace trying in vain to restore order. (The Granger Collection)

of the nation in search of a promised land of opportunity often found neither land nor opportunity.

Segregation and discrimination became national sins. It would be a century before the civil rights movement, led by Martin Luther King, Jr., and others, would force the federal government as well as the American people to fulfill the promises and accept the laws that came from the fiery ordeal of the Civil War. The stormy contest for full equality and acceptance is still being fought.

In addition to abolishing slavery in America, the Civil War also ended the belief in secession. A state that voluntarily enters the Union does not have the right to withdraw from it whenever it desires. This principle was established by the Civil War, and it was a crippling blow to the long-held belief in the power of states' rights.

National power and states' rights had too long been in conflict. Lincoln proclaimed early in his administration: "We must settle this question now, whether in a free government the minority have the right to break up the government whenever they choose." The Civil War settled that point by establishing the power of majority rule, a rule that makes our government one of the most stable on earth.

America was so strengthened by the war that Americans stopped saying "the United States are." People thought of the country as a oneness after the war and said "the United States *is*." Another new phrase came into use. "The Union" slowly came to be the term used to refer to all of the states.

Politics and economics also changed sharply as a result of the Civil War. The national government became more and more powerful during the war years, and that power has continued to increase almost without interruption.

The war also brought a dramatic shift of political power from South to North. In the early years of America, Southerners dominated the Congress and the federal courts. That is no longer true. Eight of our first eleven presidents were from the South. After 1865, it would be more than a hundred years before another lifelong Southerner, Jimmy Carter, would be elected president of the United States.

Even more apparent to the country and to the world was the complete shift in post–Civil War economic pursuits. As we have seen, the antebellum South dominated the American economy with its cotton and other

Rough wooden boards were the markers first used for soldiers' graves. This wartime photograph of Richmond's Hollywood Cemetery shows the graves of some of the Confederates who died while defending the capital. (Library of Congress)

staple crops. This was not unusual at the time. Agriculture was the economic basis for most of the world's nations.

Because of the Civil War, however, a slowly industrializing North slipped into high gear. The aptly named Industrial Revolution was in full force by war's end and picked up speed in the 1870s. Capitalism and industry have since replaced farming and agriculture as America's economic bases. The result has been to make this country the most powerful industrial nation in history.

On a lighter note, the Civil War gave rise to more new songs than any other event in our history. The first war tune appeared three days after Fort Sumter. By the time of the Appomattox surrender, 2,000 songs had been written. A few that are still popular today are "The Battle Hymn of the Republic," "When Johnny Comes Marching Home," "The Yellow Rose of Texas," "The Battle Cry of Freedom," and "Tenting Tonight on the Old Campground."

Dozens of other songs and hymns written before the Civil War gained lasting popularity because of that struggle. They include "The Star-Spangled Banner," "Home, Sweet Home," "Auld Lang Syne," "Praise God from Whom All Blessings Flow," "How Firm a Foundation," "O God, Our Help in Ages Past," "Amazing Grace," and "Sweet Hour of Prayer."

The Civil War still lives in other ways. It is "our" war—us against us. The war belongs to Americans alone and permits us to take pride in the gallantry shown on both sides. The war directly touches people today because so many citizens have at least one ancestor who fought in it.

More books have been written about the Civil War than any other subject in American history. Many battlefields are preserved, and millions of people visit them each year. Civil War monuments stand on courthouse lawns, school grounds, road intersections, and city squares. Museums, highway markers, and exhibits of all types are other reminders of a time when America was a battleground.

Soldier cemeteries stand all across the nation too. At rest in those quiet places are Northern and Southern patriots who loved their land more than they valued their lives. The United States lives because they died. If we forget that lesson of the past, we may lose the great dreams of the future.

The "War of Firsts"

No war in history produced more new ideas, weapons, and techniques than did the Civil War. How that contest was being fought in 1865 was centuries in advance of how the war was fought in 1861. As in olden days, the Civil War began with military movements being carefully kept apart from civilian life. By the last years of the conflict, armies were carrying war to the enemy's people as well as its armies.

Dozens of other things appeared for the first time in the Civil War.

New instruments of war included the rifle, rifled cannon, the machine gun, trench warfare to a degree never before seen, hand grenades, land mines, ironclad ships, attack submarines, widespread use of underwater mines, and blockades and blockade-running all along a nation's coastline.

Other Civil War "firsts" were the use of the telegraph as a military instrument; railroads as military transportation and objectives; photography in the field with the armies; drafting of Americans into the armed forces; an ambulance-wagon system for transporting wounded soldiers; military observation from a manned balloon; organized use of black soldiers; the nation's most famous bugle call, taps, and the Congressional Medal of Honor.

Behind the lines, the Civil War marked the birth of paper money, a government agency for collecting taxes, the beginning of the American Red Cross, shoes designed for left and right feet to make walking more comfortable, the first American depiction of Santa Claus, and the custom of sending flowers to a funeral.

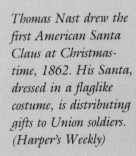

Thomas Nast drew the first American Santa Claus at Christmastime, 1862. His Santa, dressed in a flaglike costume, is distributing gifts to Union soldiers. (Harper's Weekly)

MISSOURI

Wilson's Creek
Aug. 10, 1861

Pea Ridge
Mar. 6–8, 1862

Prairie Grove
Dec. 7, 1862

ARKANSAS

Island No. 10
Apr. 8, 1862

Smithland
and Paducah
Sept. 6, 1861

Fort Henry
Feb. 6, 1862

Fort Donelson
Feb. 16, 1862

INDIANA

ILLINOIS

Richmon
Aug. 30, 18

Perryville
Oct. 8, 1862

KENTUCKY

Cumberland River

Nashville
Dec. 15–16, 1864

Franklin
Nov. 30, 1864

Murfreesboro
(Stones River)
Dec. 31, 1862–
Jan. 2, 1863

Knoxvill
under sie
Nov. 1
Dec. 4, 18

Shiloh
Apr. 6–7, 1862

TENNESSEE

Chattanooga
Nov. 24–25, 1863

Holly
Springs
Dec. 20, 1862

Corinth
Oct. 3–4, 1862

Iuka
Sept. 19–20, 1862

Tennessee River

Huntsville
Apr. 11, 1862

Chickamaug
Sept. 19–20, 1863

Mississippi River

Kennesaw
Mountain
June 27, 1864

Milliken's Bend
First victory
by black soldiers
June 7, 1863

Chickasaw Bayou
Dec. 28–29, 1862

Vicksburg
under siege
May 22–July 4, 1863

MISSISSIPPI

ALABAMA

Atlanta
occupied b
Sherman
Sept. 2, 186

GEORGIA

LOUISIANA

Baton Rouge
Aug. 5, 1862

Mobile Bay
Aug. 5, 1864

FLORIDA

New Orleans
surrenders
Apr. 29, 1862

Gulf of Mexico

CHRONOLOGY

1793
Sept.   Eli Whitney invents the cotton gin.

1821
Feb. 28   Missouri Compromise blocks extension of slavery above latitudinal line of 36°30′ north.

1831
Jan. 1   William Lloyd Garrison begins publication of *The Liberator*.

1833
Dec. 5   Abolitionist groups form American Anti-Slavery Society.

1846–1848   Victory in Mexican War makes Texas, California, and all land in between part of United States.

1849
Dec.   California Territory applies for admission to Union as free state.

1850
Jan. 29   Henry Clay introduces Compromise of 1850 to settle national issues about slavery and conflicting land claims.

1851
May   First installment of Harriet Beecher Stowe's *Uncle Tom's Cabin* appears in print.

1854
May 30   Kansas-Nebraska Act passes; opens entire nation to spread of slavery.

1856
May 22   Assault on Senator Charles Sumner in U.S. Capitol.

1857
Mar. 6   Dred Scott decision—U.S. Supreme Court rules that a slave is private property.

1859
Oct. 16–18   Abolitionist John Brown and followers raid arsenal at Harpers Ferry, Virginia, in attempt to provoke slave rebellion.
Dec. 2   Execution of John Brown at Charlestown, Virginia.

1860
Nov. 6   Abraham Lincoln elected U.S. president.
Dec. 20   South Carolina leaves the Union.

1861
Jan. 9   Mississippi leaves the Union; South Carolina batteries fire on *Star of the West*.
Jan. 10   Florida leaves the Union.
Jan. 11   Alabama leaves the Union.
Jan. 19   Georgia leaves the Union.
Jan. 26   Louisiana leaves the Union.
Feb. 1   Texas leaves the Union.
Feb. 4   Confederate States of America formed in Montgomery, Alabama.
Feb. 9   Jefferson Davis elected president of the Confederacy.
Apr. 14   Fort Sumter, South Carolina, falls to Southern forces.
Apr. 15   Lincoln issues call for 75,000 troops.

Apr. 17	Virginia leaves the Union.		**1862**	
Apr. 18	Virginia militia seizes Harpers Ferry.		*Feb. 6*	Grant captures Fort Henry, Tennessee.
Apr. 19	Lincoln declares blockade of Southern ports; 6th Massachusetts attacked by civilians while passing through Baltimore, Maryland.		*Feb. 8*	Federals occupy Roanoke Island, North Carolina.
			Feb. 16	Union forces seize Fort Donelson, Tennessee.
Apr. 20	Virginia forces occupy U.S. naval base at Norfolk.		*Feb. 23*	Nashville, Tennessee, falls to Federal troops.
May 6	Arkansas leaves the Union.		*Mar. 6–8*	Federal victory at Pea Ridge, Arkansas.
May 8	Confederate capital moved to Richmond, Virginia.		*Mar. 9*	USS *Monitor* and CSS *Virginia* fight first battle between ironclad ships; neither can destroy the other.
May 10–11	Attempts by Confederates to take St. Louis, Missouri, fail.			
May 13	Federal troops occupy Baltimore, Maryland.		*Mar. 23*	Stonewall Jackson's Shenandoah Valley Campaign begins with battle at Kernstown, Virginia.
May 20	North Carolina leaves the Union.			
May 27	General Irvin McDowell placed in command of all Federal forces in and around Washington, D.C.		*Apr. 6–7*	Union victory at Shiloh, Tennessee; Confederate general A. Sidney Johnston killed, later replaced by Braxton Bragg.
June 17	Union victory at Boonville, Missouri.			
June 24	Tennessee leaves the Union.		*Apr. 8*	Island No. 10, Confederate garrison on Mississippi River, falls to Northern troops.
July 21	Confederate victory at First Manassas (First Bull Run), Virginia.			
			Apr. 11	Federal naval expedition occupies Fort Pulaski, Georgia.
July 22	General George B. McClellan replaces Irvin McDowell as commander of Union forces in the East.		*Apr. 29*	New Orleans surrenders to Union forces.
			May 5	Fighting in McClellan's Peninsular Campaign begins with drawn battle at Williamsburg, Virginia.
Aug. 10	Confederate victory at Wilson's Creek, Missouri.			
Sept. 3–4	Columbus, Kentucky, occupied by Confederates.		*May 11*	CSS *Virginia* destroyed by her crew to prevent capture.
Sept. 6	Ulysses S. Grant's Federals seize Paducah and Smithland, Kentucky.			
Sept. 12–20	Siege of Federal garrison at Lexington, Missouri.			
Sept. 16–17	Union detachment seizes Ship Island, Mississippi.			
Oct. 24	Delegates in western Virginia pass a measure calling for independent statehood.			
Nov. 7	Federals capture Port Royal, South Carolina; neither side wins battle at Belmont, Missouri.			

U. S. Army buttons. (Private collection)

Confederate sleeve badges. (Private collection)

GENERAL   COLONEL   CAPTAIN

May 31	McClellan's advance stopped by Confederates at Seven Pines, Virginia.
June 1	Robert E. Lee appointed commander of Army of Northern Virginia after General Joseph E. Johnston is wounded.
June 6	Union gunboats force surrender of Memphis, Tennessee.
June 9	Jackson's victory at Port Republic, Virginia, brings Confederates final success in Shenandoah Valley Campaign.
June 11–14	Jeb Stuart's "Ride around McClellan."
June 26	Confederate attack against McClellan at Mechanicsville, Virginia; action starts Seven Days' Campaign.
June 27	Lee's forces defeat Federals at Gaines's Mill.
June 30	Fighting at White Oak Swamp and Frayser's Farm, Virginia, fails to stop Union retreat toward James River.
July 1	McClellan wins battle of Malvern Hill, Virginia; Seven Days' Campaign ends with Richmond still unconquered.
Aug. 5	Federals beat back attacks at Baton Rouge, Louisiana.
Aug. 6	CSS *Arkansas* destroyed in naval battle on Mississippi River.
Aug. 9	Jackson defeats Federals at Cedar Mountain, Virginia.
Aug. 28–30	Confederates triumph at Second Manassas (Second Bull Run), Virginia.
Aug. 30	Confederates seize Richmond, Kentucky.
Sept. 15	Confederates capture garrison of 12,000 Federals at Harpers Ferry.
Sept. 17	Bloodiest one-day battle of the war at Antietam Creek, Maryland, stops Lee's advance into the North; in Kentucky, Confederates force surrender of Federal post at Munfordville.
Sept. 19–20	Federal victory at Iuka, Mississippi.
Sept. 22	Lincoln announces plans to issue Emancipation Proclamation.
Sept. 30	Confederate attacks beaten back at Newtonia, Missouri.
Oct. 3–4	Federals win battle for Corinth, Mississippi.
Oct. 8	Confederate defeat at Perryville, Kentucky.
Oct. 30	General William S. Rosecrans replaces Don Carlos Buell in command of Federal forces in Tennessee.
Nov. 7	McClellan removed from command of Federal army; succeeded by Ambrose E. Burnside.
Dec. 7	Union forces victorious in fighting at Prairie Grove, Arkansas.
Dec. 13	Lee wins one-sided battle at Fredericksburg, Virginia.
Dec. 20	Grant's supply base destroyed at Holly Springs, Mississippi.
Dec. 28–29	Federals defeated at Chickasaw Bayou, Mississippi.
Dec. 31	Three-day battle of Murfreesboro

(Stones River), Tennessee, begins; USS *Monitor* lost at sea.

1863

Jan. 1   Emancipation Proclamation frees all slaves in Confederate states.

Jan. 26   General Joseph Hooker replaces Burnside as commander of the Union's Army of the Potomac.

Mar. 5   General Bedford Forrest routs Federals at Thompson's Station, Tennessee.

Mar. 25   Forrest wins engagement at Brentwood, Tennessee.

Apr. 20   Another victory for Forrest at Franklin, Tennessee.

May 1   Grant seizes Port Gibson, Mississippi.

May 2–5   Lee victorious in heavy fighting at Chancellorsville, Virginia; Stonewall Jackson mortally wounded.

May 3   Federal reinforcements moving toward Chancellorsville defeated at Salem Church, Virginia.

May 12   Grant wins battle of Raymond, Mississippi.

May 14   Grant victorious at Jackson, Mississippi.

May 16   Another Union victory at Champion's Hill, Mississippi.

May 22   Grant's second attempt to seize Vicksburg fails; Federal siege of the city begins.

May 27   Black troops see first action in Federal defeat at Port Hudson, Louisiana.

June 7   Defeat of Confederates at Milliken's Bend, Louisiana, gives black soldiers their first victory.

June 20   West Virginia admitted to the Union.

June 28   Union general Hooker replaced by General George G. Meade.

Medicine chest.
(Private collection)

July 1–3   Pickett's Charge ends battle of Gettysburg, Pennsylvania, and brings first major Union victory in the East; hard-pressed Confederates abandon supply base at Tullahoma, Tennessee.

July 4   Vicksburg, Mississippi, surrenders to Grant; Mississippi River now under Federal control.

July 9   Port Hudson, Louisiana, falls to Federals.

July 18   Federal assault force with all-black 54th Massachusetts defeated at Fort Wagner, South Carolina.

Sept. 19–20   Chickamauga Campaign, Georgia, results in victory for Southern forces.

Oct. 14   Federals beat back attack at Bristoe Station, Virginia.

Nov. 17   Confederate siege of Knoxville, Tennessee, begins.

Nov. 24–25   Federal victories at Lookout Mountain and Missionary Ridge, Tennessee.

Revolvers.
(Private collection)

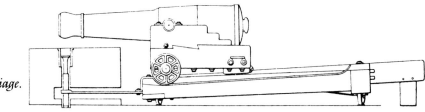

Wooden artillery carriage.
(Private collection)

Nov. 26	Four-day campaign of maneuvers begins at Mine Run, Virginia; no major fighting.
Dec. 1	Bragg resigns as commander of the South's Army of Tennessee; later succeeded by Joseph E. Johnston.
Dec. 4	Confederate siege of Knoxville, Tennessee, ends in defeat for Southerners.

1864

Feb. 17	Confederate submarine *Hunley* sinks USS *Housatonic* and itself.
Mar. 9	Grant takes command of all Federal armies.
Mar. 18	Sherman assumes command of all Federal forces in the West.
May 5–6	Battle of the Wilderness, Virginia, is a sharp setback for Federals.
May 5–19	Federal general Benjamin Butler's campaign to seize Richmond by way of the James River fails.
May 7	Sherman begins campaign to capture Atlanta, Georgia.
May 9–12	Federal general Sheridan's cavalry raid toward Richmond causes much damage.
May 9–19	Grant's second attempt to get around Lee's flank fails in fighting around Spotsylvania, Virginia.
May 11	Confederate cavalry chief Jeb Stuart mortally wounded at Yellow Tavern, Virginia.
May 15	Federals under General Franz Sigel routed at New Market, Virginia.

May 21	General David Hunter replaces Sigel in command of Federal forces in the Shenandoah Valley.
May 23–26	Sharp fighting along the North Anna River, Virginia, persuades Grant to try another approach to Richmond.
June 3	Grant suffers his worst defeat of the war at Cold Harbor, Virginia.
June 11	Lexington, Virginia, seized and much of it burned by Hunter's Federal army.
June 15–18	First Petersburg Campaign, Virginia; Federals defeated, but Grant determines to lay siege to the city.
June 16–19	Hunter's Federal advance stopped at Lynchburg, Virginia.
June 19	CSS *Alabama* sunk by USS *Kearsarge* off French coast.
June 27	Sherman defeated at Kennesaw Mountain, Georgia.
July 17	Johnston relieved of command of Atlanta defense forces; replaced by General John B. Hood.
July 20	Confederate attack at Peachtree Creek, Georgia, fails.
July 22	Confederate attack at Atlanta, Georgia, also fails.
July 28	Union victory at Ezra Church, Georgia.
Aug. 5	Farragut's naval victory at Mobile Bay, Alabama.
Aug. 6	Hunter replaced by General Philip Sheridan as Federal commander of troops in western Virginia.

Aug. 31	Confederates defeated at Jonesboro, Georgia: Hood abandons city.
Sept. 2	Sherman occupies Atlanta, Georgia.
Sept. 19	Federals break enemy lines at Opequon Creek, Virginia.
Sept. 22	Sheridan's Union forces victorious at Fisher's Hill, Virginia.
Oct. 19	Sheridan's victory at Cedar Creek, Virginia, gives Federals control of the Shenandoah Valley.
Oct. 27–28	CSS *Albemarle* destroyed by Federal raiding party.
Nov. 8	Lincoln reelected president of the United States.
Nov. 15	Sherman sets fire to Atlanta and begins March to the Sea across Georgia.
Nov. 30	Confederate slaughter at Franklin, Tennessee.
Dec. 15–16	Federal victory at Nashville, Tennessee; Hood asks to be relieved of command.
Dec. 22	Sherman "reaches the sea" at Savannah, Georgia.

1865

Jan. 31	Lee appointed general in chief of all Confederate armies.
Feb. 1	Sherman begins "March through the Carolinas."
Feb. 17	Columbia, South Carolina, surrenders to Sherman.
Feb. 18	Union troops occupy Charleston, South Carolina.
Feb. 22	Fall of Wilmington, North Carolina; Joseph E. Johnston appointed to command of all Southern forces in the Carolinas.
Mar. 4	Lincoln's second inauguration.
Mar. 11	Sherman occupies Fayetteville, North Carolina.
Mar. 19–21	Confederate attacks unsuccessful at Bentonville, North Carolina.

Mar. 25	Union victory at Fort Stedman, Virginia.
Apr. 1	Grant breaks Lee's lines at Five Forks.
Apr. 2	Lee abandons Petersburg and Richmond, then retreats westward.
Apr. 3	Federal forces march into Richmond.
Apr. 6	Union victory at Sayler's Creek, Virginia.
Apr. 9	Lee surrenders at Appomattox Court House, Virginia.
Apr. 14	Lincoln murdered at Ford's Theater in Washington.
Apr. 26	Confederate general J. E. Johnston surrenders Army of Tennessee at Bennett Place, North Carolina.
May 4	Surrender of Confederate forces in Alabama and Mississippi.
May 10	Jefferson Davis captured at Irwinville, Georgia.
May 26	Confederate troops west of the Mississippi surrender.
Nov. 6	CSS *Shenandoah* lowers the last Confederate flag.
Dec. 18	Adoption of Thirteenth Amendment; prohibits slavery in the United States.

1867

Mar. 2	Military Reconstruction Act passed; Southern states placed under martial law.

1868

July 28	Adoption of Fourteenth Amendment; promises equality to all U.S. citizens.

1870

Mar. 30	Adoption of Fifteenth Amendment; guarantees right to vote for every male American citizen regardless of color.

GLOSSARY

Abolitionists People who wanted to end slavery.

Antebellum period The years 1820–1860, when King Cotton ruled the South and abolitionists became powerful in the North.

Artillery The big guns (cannon and mortars) in an army; in the Civil War, artillery was used mainly to support infantry charges and defend fixed positions.

Blockade The practice of positioning naval ships in front of an enemy's harbors and river openings to prevent vessels loaded with commerce from entering and departing.

Breastworks Defensive positions of dirt and wood. Such works were chest-high, which gave some protection for soldiers firing at the enemy.

Brevet promotion A temporary rise in rank, usually given in wartime for brave or outstanding service in the line of duty.

Cavalry Soldiers mounted on horses and used primarily for scouting and raids.

Colors The flag or banner of a military unit.

Confederates Southern soldiers, also called Johnny Rebs and butternuts (because their homemade uniforms were light tan).

Confederation A combination of independent states with a central government having only those powers given to it by the member states.

Conscription Laws by which men were ordered into military service; today it is called the draft.

Cotton gin The machine that made harvesting cotton easier; it was invented by Eli Whitney in 1793.

Cotton Kingdom The South during the years 1820–1860.

Diarrhea A name for several kinds of intestinal illnesses resulting largely from bad food; diarrhea was the biggest killer in the Civil War.

Earthworks Trenches with wooden frameworks and dirt in front; traces of these fortifications still exist on many battlefields.

Emancipation Proclamation President Lincoln's order that, as of January 1, 1863, all slaves in any state that had not returned to the Union by then would be free.

Federals Union soldiers, also called Billy Yanks and bluecoats.

Federation A government in which each member state gives supreme power to the central authority.

Flank The end of a battle line, such as the left flank or the western flank.

Free-Soilers People opposed to the spread of slavery beyond the South; also called anti-slaveryites.

Garrisonians Militant abolitionists who regarded slavery as a sin to be destroyed by any means. The name came from the leader of this group, William Lloyd Garrison.

Hardtack A large square cracker that was the bread ration in Union armies; so-called because it could be hard enough to break teeth.

Industrial Revolution The nineteenth-century development in which machinery, power tools,

Medicine wagon. (Private collection)

and large-scale production replaced handmade techniques and small factories.

Infantry Soldiers trained and equipped to fight on foot; the basic unit of a Civil War army.

Inflation A sharp increase of money in circulation, which decreases the buying power of money and increases the price of goods and services.

Ironclad A naval vessel covered above the water line with iron plating.

Matériel Equipment and supplies for waging war.

Ordnance Military weapons and the supplies necessary to operate them.

Overseer In the Cotton Kingdom, the supervisor who bossed slaves at work in the fields.

Parole The practice of allowing captured soldiers to return home on their promise not to fight again.

"Peculiar institution" A Southern term for slavery.

Piedmont The rolling hill country in Virginia and the Carolinas between the Allegheny Mountains and the flat tidewater region near the Atlantic coast.

Popular sovereignty A widespread belief in the 1850s that only the residents of a territory should decide whether that territory should be a free state or a slave state.

Rebellion A war in which part of the people of a country try to overthrow the government and establish a new ruling power.

"Red badge of courage" A battle wound.

Regiment The basic army unit of that time; a Civil War regiment was supposed to consist of one thousand men (ten companies of a hundred soldiers each), but sickness and losses kept the size to about half that.

Rifling A spiral groove inside a gun barrel. The groove made the bullet spin, thus giving it greater range and accuracy.

Secession The act whereby a state formally leaves the United States of America; the federal government (i.e., the government in Washington, D.C.) considers secession to be illegal.

Siege A military operation in which an army surrounds or pins down the enemy force, cuts communications and supply lines, and slowly starves the enemy into surrender.

Springfield musket The most popular shoulder weapon of that day; it became more effective after rifling was done to the inside of the barrel.

States' rights The political doctrine that all powers not specifically given to the federal government by the U.S. Constitution belong to a state.

Theater A large area where military campaigns took place; in the Civil War there were three main theaters: eastern, western, and trans-Mississippi.

Torpedoes Stationary underwater mines used for protecting rivers and harbor channels.

Swords and sabers. (Private collection)

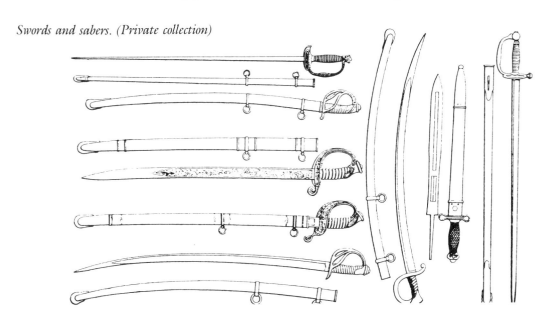

FOR FURTHER READING

Titles with an asterisk (*) are books written especially for children.

GENERAL WORKS

Catton, Bruce, *The American Heritage Picture History of the Civil War* (American Heritage, 1960). Still one of the most popular of all Civil War books.

——, *The Centennial History of the Civil War* (3 vols., Doubleday, 1961–1965). A beautifully written history of the struggle.

——, *This Hallowed Ground* (Doubleday, 1962). Written by the master Civil War storyteller, this account treats only the Northern side.

*Cross, Helen Reeder, *Life in Lincoln's America* (Random House, 1964). An illustrated history of the nation in the 1860s.

Davis, William C. (ed.), *The Image of War, 1861–1865* (5 vols., Doubleday, 1981–1983). The largest of the modern picture-histories of the Civil War.

Henry, Robert Selph, *The Story of the Confederacy* (Bobbs-Merrill, 1931). An old but readable account of the Confederate States.

McPherson, James M., *Battle Cry of Freedom: The Civil War Era* (Oxford University Press, 1988). The most popular history in the field today.

Roland, Charles P., *An American Iliad* (McGraw-Hill, 1990). An extremely well written general history of the war.

Ward, Geoffrey C., *The Civil War: An Illustrated History* (Knopf, 1990). A fresh collection of pictures based on a popular television series.

BATTLES AND ARMIES

Catton, Bruce, *Mr. Lincoln's Army; Glory Road; A Stillness at Appomattox* (Doubleday, 1951–1953). The fullest history of the Army of the Potomac; told mostly from within the ranks.

Freeman, Douglas S., *Lee's Lieutenants: A Study in Command* (3 vols., Scribners, 1942–1944). The most detailed history of the Army of Northern Virginia ever likely to be written.

Horn, Stanley F., *The Army of Tennessee* (University of Oklahoma Press, 1953). Useful for a good look at the Confederacy's second major army.

*Kantor, MacKinlay, *Gettysburg* (Random House, 1952). A better-than-average battle narrative for young readers.

Macdonald, John, *Great Battles of the Civil War* (Macmillan, 1988). This large volume, with many illustrations (including computerized drawings), examines eighteen major battles of the war.

Robertson, James I., Jr., *Civil War Sites in Virginia: A Tour Guide* (University Press of Virginia, 1982). Provides summaries, keyed maps, and road directions for the major battlefields and Civil War scenes in the state.

Sears, Stephen W., *Landscape Turned Red: The Battle of Antietam* (Ticknor & Fields, 1983). The most complete treatment of the bloodiest one-day engagement of the war.

Sword, Wiley, *Shiloh: Bloody April* (Morrow, 1974). By far the most thorough study of that battle.

*Symonds, Craig L., *A Battlefield Atlas of the Civil War* (Nautical and Aviation Publishing Co., 1983). Full-page maps and narrative of the major campaigns.

Wheeler, Richard, *Sherman's March* (Cromwell, 1978). The campaign from Atlanta to the Atlantic, told in the words of those who were part of it and victims of it.

LEADERS OF NORTH AND SOUTH

*Daniels, Jonathan, *Robert E. Lee* (Houghton Mifflin, 1960). An excellent introduction to the South's most famous soldier.

Eaton, Clement, *Jefferson Davis* (Free Press, 1977).

The most recent of several biographies of the misunderstood president.

* Freedman, Russell, *Lincoln: A Photobiography* (Clarion Books, 1987). An outstanding introduction to the Northern chief executive.

* Fritz, Jean, *Stonewall* (Putnam, 1979). Covers the high points in the life of General Thomas J. Jackson.

McFeely, William S., *Grant: A Biography* (Norton, 1981). Thorough in both facts and interpretations.

Merrill, James M., *William Tecumseh Sherman* (Rand McNally, 1971). This balanced treatment contains many quotations by and about the general.

Warner, Ezra J., *Generals in Blue* (Louisiana State University Press, 1964). Biographical sketches and photographs of every Union general.

———, *Generals in Gray* (Louisiana State University Press, 1959). The same for Confederate field commanders.

Williams, T. Harry, *Lincoln Finds a General* (Knopf, 1952). Tells of the president's search for a winning team.

SLAVERY

* Evitts, William J., *Captive Bodies, Free Spirits: The Story of Southern Slavery* (Julian Messner, 1985). An introduction to a complicated subject.

Stampp, Kenneth M., *The Imperiled Union* (Oxford University Press, 1980). New interpretations of slavery and the antebellum South.

* Sterling, Dorothy, *Forever Free: The Story of the Emancipation Proclamation* (Doubleday, 1963). A far-ranging history of the American slave's road to freedom.

Wiley, Bell I., *Southern Negroes, 1861–1865* (Rinehart, 1938). A scholarly survey of slave life inside the Confederacy.

SPECIALIZED STUDIES

Adams, George W., *Doctors in Blue* (Schuman, 1952). A solid survey of Union medical treatment.

* Colby, C. B., *Civil War Weapons* (Coward-McCann, 1962). Photographs and word descriptions of the major weapons used.

Cornish, Dudley T., *The Sable Arm: Black Troops in the Union Army, 1861–1865* (Longmans, Green, 1956). The basic reference for black soldiers in the war.

Cunningham, H. H., *Doctors in Gray* (Louisiana State University Press, 1958). The only scholarly work on Confederate medicine.

* Donovan, Frank R., *Ironclads of the Civil War* (American Heritage, 1964). A word-and-picture chronicle of the naval war.

Hesseltine, William B., *Civil War Prisons* (Ohio State University Press, 1930). The only scholarly work on a highly emotional subject.

Massey, Mary Elizabeth, *Bonnet Brigades* (Knopf, 1966). An outstanding study of women in the Civil War.

Robertson, James I., Jr., *Civil War Virginia: Battleground for a Nation* (University Press of Virginia, 1991). A wide-ranging summary of events and people in the war's most pivotal state.

———, *Soldiers Blue and Gray* (University of South Carolina Press, 1988). Army life in the Civil War, as told for the most part by Johnny Rebs and Billy Yanks themselves.

Six-mule team hitched to U.S. Army wagon. (Private collection)

INDEX